THE EDUCATIONAL THOUGHT OF THE CLASSICAL POLITICAL ECONOMISTS

Margaret G. O'Donnell

UNIVERSITY
PRESS OF
AMERICA

LANHAM • NEW YORK • LONDON

University Press of America,® Inc.

4720 Boston Way
Lanham, MD 20706

3 Henrietta Street
London WC2E 8LU England

Library of Congress Cataloging in Publication Data

O'Donnell, Margaret G., 1943-
    The educational thought of the classical political
economists.

    Includes index.
    1. Education —Philosophy—History. 2. Education—
Economic aspects—Europe—History.   3. Classical
school of economics—History.   4. Education and state—
Europe—History. I. Title.
LA123.036   1985   370'.1   85-13487
ISBN 0-8191-4817-2 (alk. paper)
ISBN 0-8191-4818-0 (pbk. : alk. paper)

To my family

Table of Contents

Preface

Preface

The idea for this book was the result of a combination of interests. My basic interests lie in the history of economic thought, but over the years, I have become involved to some extent with economic education. This involvement led me to wonder about the place of education in the minds of the economic thinkers of long ago.

As I began researching this topic, I became aware of the fact that a classical economist's position on education could not be isolated from his more fundamental beliefs. The classical thinkers wrote at a crucial time in the formation of modern economic systems. They could choose to hold fast to the laissez-faire ideas of old or they could opt to rethink their economic philosophy in terms of the needs of a new era. A specific economist's thoughts on education, universal education, state involvement in education, compulsory attendance legislation and myriad other questions concerning the educational experience were typical of his feelings about the economic system which he felt to be best for the future of society. Consequently, this investigation took on a broader interpretation. I was looking for an economist's thoughts on education and educational plans but I was finding these things as extensions of the economist's basic beliefs and also of the tone of the times.

Research into the history of economic ideas, as any other research, requires data gathering. The data which are accumulated here are not figures that fit into formulas but are the thoughts of previous writers. Accuracy demands that the ideas of these thinkers be reproduced verbatim as much as possible. Just as the number "twenty-seven" does not lend itself to verbal reconstruction, I believe that a writer's words should not be liberally reconstructed to "say" what he may or may not have said. Therefore, this book is chock full of quotations. These quotations will demonstrate what the author did write and not how a second party interpreted his words.

Some classical writers were more systematic in their thinking than others and considered a discussion of educational problems essential to a thorough treatment of political economy. Some classicals were encouraged by the social and economic problems of their day to speak their minds about the place that they believed education held in solving these problems. In these writings, the author's "theory" of education can be unearthed. Other classicals did not treat a discussion of education as essential to their main theses but mentioned it tangentially. These casual observations should not be overlooked, however, since they often contained the kernel of an educational idea which bloomed at a later date.

This research was begun when I was the recipient of an Institute of Humane Studies Summer Research Fellowship. I would like to thank the Institute for giving me the opportunity to become involved in this project. I would also like to thank my friend and colleague, Tony Greco, for his comments on an earlier draft of this manuscript.

CHAPTER I

AN INTRODUCTION TO THE EDUCATION OF
EIGHTEENTH AND NINETEENTH CENTURY EUROPE

INTRODUCTION

The eighteenth and nineteenth centuries in Europe were fraught with economic change. The rapid rise of technology demanded a literate work force as an absolute minimum. It was essential that the worker be able to read instructions, perform simple calculations, and be adaptable enough to respond quickly to the ever changing work environment. Over time, increases in worker education did occur and resulted in increases in worker productivity; however, the growing need for technical knowledge demanded changes both in the quantity of and in the quality of the education offered.

Early political economists sought to describe the resource relationships which blended together in the production process. The introduction of sophisticated machinery into the work place caused a rise in labor productivity but, at the same time, required that employees be more highly skilled. Adding "quality" to the resource labor opened up a new dimension in the microeconomic determination of the rewards to the factors of production. Additionally, the availability of opportunities for workers to increase their level of "quality" led to new interpretations of the idea of justice.

On the macroeconomic level, national policy makers believed that commercial success could be expanded into national advantage and that, eventually, national advantage would lead to international supremacy. Consequently, the skill level and the educational attainment of a nation's citizens were no longer a matter of individual achievement or even a matter of competitive advantage for a single firm. Moreover, it was recognized that a high level of national production not only affected a nation's relative position in the economic world, but it also yielded a high level of employment which had a positive effect on individual health and happiness. This effect was compounded over all workers and the total level of national well-being rose as output increased. Many held that the social and humanitarian returns to high employment were even greater than the economic. These benefits were cited as accruing directly to the dissemination of education among the masses; this made education a fit subject for national policy making.

The political economists of the nineteenth century were often involved in the formulation of the educational policy which was

1

being created.[1] For the most part, they were teachers who wielded substantial influence in their respective universities; but, in addition, they were noted authors whose ideas commanded popular trust and whose works were liberally discussed throughout the intellectual community. Many of these economists were directly involved with policy making through their positions in government or as consultants to elected officials. Sometimes their ideas were politically acceptable and surfaced in new educational policy. However, often they wrote in opposition to the established educational plan, sometimes with success, but more often without it.

The economists commented on the educational supply problems of their day. They were struck by the fact that generally the supply of education to the common people in most European countries in the 1700s and 1800s was lamentable. Teachers were usually ignorant men and women who could not succeed at any other occupation.[2] Often teaching was the schoolmaster's secondary trade, as in parish or dame schools.[3] Here the children were set up in a living room or workshop where the lessons were taught while the instructor engaged in another line of work.[4] In these ungraded schools the three "R's" were reading, writing, and religion. Arithmetic was judged too difficult to master. By the age of ten or eleven, the child's education was considered complete.

The education of the ordinary man was restricted to the little that he could absorb in these schools for small children. Young men who had higher ambitions and whose parents could afford the expense were sent to secondary or grammar schools.[5] Often these were endowed schools which were funded by deceased benefactors and which held fast to the terms of their endowments. Typically a religious creed was specified in endowed schools. The most common type of secondary school was the traditional Latin school which was noted for its formal unchanging curriculum, and generally spiritless instruction.[6] Since the education received in these grammar schools originally prepared pupils for the learned professions, especially the Church and the law, the study of Latin and Greek was essential to the students' future occupations.[7] Over time, these educational institutions were called on to supply the educational needs of a complex society. The classical tradition of these schools became increasingly out of touch with the practical needs of the pupils.[8]

Most of the classical political economists were products of the secondary schools and had used the knowledge gained there to enter the university. Sometimes they were trained for professions for which they had no personal preference, simply because of the static nature of higher education which restricted their study to traditional subjects. Very often these writers were the strongest advocates of changes within the educational system.

2

Frustrated by the wasted years spent in the study of irrelevant subjects, these authors specified the elements of a useful secondary curriculum. Knowing that a secondary education rests on the primary instruction received, they also identified the basic substance of a firm foundation of elementary work in the lower school.

The demand for education in eighteenth and nineteenth century Europe was varied depending upon the income class of the student's parents. The wealthy student could easily be taught an elementary course of study by a private tutor at home, then progress to a traditional secondary school for additional training which prepared him to enter the university. Often the secondary school was a boarding school, which minimized attendance problems. At the university level, absenteeism was common and, especially in France, had reached shameful proportions.[9] Furthermore, the attendance rates in all schools, at all levels, left doubts about the seriousness of the demand for education among the rich as well as the poor.

The children of working class parents were those who frequented the dame schools to learn their letters. Their education was generally characterized by a special attendance problem. These students left school when their income as factory workers became crucial to the support of their families. If the family could afford to forego a child's contribution to the household's income, and if the child were especially gifted, he might proceed to a secondary trade school or to an endowed school on a tuition scholarship. The student would usually round out his education by serving an apprenticeship in a skilled trade.

Finally, the demand for education was weakest among the poorest classes. The need to send even the youngest children into the factories or fields to work often precluded the most rudimentary instruction. Children who had to show certification of school attendance to obtain work habitually forged the certificates or conspired with the factory owners to skirt the regulations. Parents of the poorest children felt hostile toward the educational system and encouraged their children to avoid school. These parents felt that their children would be educated to regard them with contempt and to detest their lot in life. They judged that, for their children, no school was preferable to attending the schools then offered to them.

The financing of education was rapidly changing through the eighteenth and nineteenth centuries. The earliest suppliers of education had been representatives of religious groups. These were soon joined by nonreligious suppliers who thought that teaching should not stress any particular religious doctrine. Private schools for wealthy or for middle class students were supported by fees assessed to cover the costs of running the school. In schools for pauper children, voluntary contributions originally provided enough funding to supply a minimum level of education for this socio-economic group. However, as the years passed, it became obvious that the number of poor and working class children in need of education far outstripped the funding ability of philanthropists. In addition, the presence of religious dogma in the pauper schools often caused parents to avoid them altogether. Therefore, the cry for state involvement in and financial aid to education was raised. It was bolstered by the growing conviction that education of the masses held the key to future national prosperity and individual happiness. The different countries of Europe responded differently to the cry for the state in education. Some recognized the need early and set the required legislation in motion; others ignored the call for as long as possible.

SCOTCH EDUCATION

The concept of universal elementary education was promoted in Scotland as early as 1560. The Scottish Reformers in their First Book of Discipline promulgated the idea of a school in every town and a schoolmaster in every parish.[10] This notion was legalized in 1696 upon passage by the Scotch Parliament of legislation calling for every parish to supply a "commodious house for a school" and the salary for a teacher.[11]

When Scotsman, Adam Smith, wrote his *Wealth of Nations* in 1776, the intentions of the 17th century Parliament had not yet been fulfilled. The early legislation had not specified the source of funds for the school or for the teacher's salary and, therefore, compliance with the law was left up to the munificence of the inhabitants of each parish. When Smith wrote, Scotch education was neither free nor compulsory, although the state had formally acknowledged the social benefits of its widespread provision. However, by 1872, universal education was effectively established when local authorities were given the power to levy rates. It is noteworthy that this regulation followed a suggestion of Smith and compelled the individual to attain knowledge, not to attend school. In evidence of the required knowledge level, a child was exempted from school attendance if he or she could read, write and show knowledge of elementary arithmetic.[12]

GERMAN EDUCATION

In legislation passed in 1794, Prussia, the largest German state, was first to identify the education of children as a legal function of the state, and not of parents or of the church.[13]

4

Only twenty years later, the country's Bureau of Education was raised to the level of a national Department of Education, indicating the rapid rise in the need for additional administrative involvement to meet the expanded state educational role. Also, to broaden the educational power base, local church school boards were replaced with provincial school boards at this time.[14] The compulsory education law became effective by 1840 when the national primary schools received financing through local taxes. It has been estimated that most German children by 1885 were receiving eight years of primary school education in the Volksschulen.[15] These elementary schools were free, although as late as 1888, pupils who could afford to pay were assessed small fees.[16]

Karl Marx wrote during an era when compulsory universal education provided by the state was an established idea in Germany. Nevertheless, Marx observed quality differences in the state supplied education of his day. Marx remained dissatisfied with the educational system even though the German schools were judged to be truly innovative and had had a tradition of teaching "practical" subjects. In spite of the fact that the German state had introduced the Realgymnasium in 1744 which emphasized scientific and technical rather than linguistic subjects, Marx still challenged the German state to provide the genuine type of education that he perceived was needed for the future of society.[17]

Another German writer, Wilhelm von Humboldt, also felt that German education was not living up to its potential. Humboldt was in a position to bring about the necessary changes when, as Minister of Education, he reorganized the German schools of higher education in 1809. Additionally, he established a new university in Berlin which became a prototype for such institutions worldwide. Special features of this university included research and graduate departments which studied nontraditional subjects. Realizing that the secondary schools produced the students who matriculated at the university, Humboldt became instrumental in reforming the secondary schools of Germany as well.[18]

FRENCH EDUCATION

Early French education was provided by Catholic brothers and priests. First LaSalle and the Christian Brothers and then the Jesuits supplied education to the young children of France. But in 1762, after nearly a century of educational provision, the Jesuit schools were closed, leaving a void that opened the way for early state interference.

France led the Continent in novel educational thinking in the mid 1700s and Jean Jacques Rousseau's *Emile* rapidly became the

5

most influential book on education in Europe.[19] In *Emile* Rousseau took the nature of the child into account, believing that individuals treated as individuals learn more effectively. He also strongly supported national education in France. These two educational ideas were both new and popularly appealing, especially in France which was filled with prerevolutionary zeal. Curiously, Adam Smith was traveling in Europe when the question of national education was being actively discussed. Smith listened to the opinions of his French contemporaries and willingly admitted the benefits of popular education. However, he was disinclined to accept the same educational solutions as the French or Germans.[20]

After the Revolution of 1789, the cry for national education was louder than ever. The French Constitution of 1791 declared that the state should organize a "public school system that was to be the same for all citizens, free, and consisting of the teaching of such subjects as the educators regarded necessary for all men."[21] Economist Jean Baptist Say expressed the strong French sentiment toward national education when he wrote *A Treatise on Political Economy* in 1803. In this work he avowed his belief in the power of governmentally supplied education to yield maximum social advance. Additionally, the popular optimism of the French Revolution and its faith in government alternatives were well represented in Say's educational ideas.

Within a short time these lofty revolutionary convictions were perverted by Napoleon's policies. Oddly enough, Napoleon agreed that "of all political questions that (of education) is perhaps the most important."[22] But Napoleon's idea of educational importance was demonstrated when he founded the University of France in 1806, which was a merger of all the institutions of higher learning in the country. The law which established the University allowed it to exercise monopoly control over education. The act read in part: "no one may open a school or teach publicly unless he is a member of the imperial university and a graduate of one of its faculties... . No school may set up outside the university and without the sanction of its head."[23] To Napoleon's additional discredit, there was no provision in the legislation of this time for upgrading or expanding the elementary school system.

Claude Frederic Bastiat wrote around 1845 responding to the dictatorial educational policies of Napoleon. He solidly objected to the state monopoly over education and accused the state of gross resource mismanagement. Bastiat felt that governmental intervention in education was not only unjust but was also marginally immoral. He was outraged at the politicizing of education under Napoleon.

Nevertheless, within the first half of the nineteenth century, the French government enacted a national system of primary education and passed legislation to allow the operation of private and parochial schools once again.[24]   Much of the impetus for the national legislation came from local groups who were demanding more schools.[25]   As the century came to a close, French legislators passed the Ferry Law of 1882 which established an effective system of free and compulsory education.[26]   Moreover, by that time, the university system had undergone a complete reorganization.

ENGLISH EDUCATION

In England, as in France, the earliest attempt at basic universal education was the product of the efforts of competing religious groups.   The Society for Promoting Christian Knowledge (SPCK), founded by Thomas Bray in 1698, maintained a fairly wide network of charity schools "in each parish and about London."[27]   The stated aim of these schools was the elimination of vice and degradation among the lower classes, although at least in part, the schools were to constitute "little garrisons against Popery" countering the established Jesuit institutions.[28]   After forty years of operation the SPCK had achieved no small measure of success.   It claimed responsibility for two thousand schools in England and Wales and for the education of forty thousand scholars.   The work of the SPCK was supplemented by the efforts of the Society for the Support and Encouragement of Sunday Schools in the Different Counties of England formed by Robert Raikes in 1785.   Raikes concentrated his efforts on the education of children who worked during the week.[29]

By the beginning of the nineteenth century, impoverished British children were educated by still other social minded groups which had been founded to encourage the spread of literacy. The two major educational organizations of the time were the National Society for Promoting the Education of the Poor in the Principles of the Church of England and the multi-denominational British and Foreign Schools Society.[30]   The monitorial schools opened by these societies followed the teaching techniques of Joseph Lancaster who first introduced his teaching methodology in a school for poor children in London in 1798.[31]   Lancaster boasted that his system could teach a hundred pupils using "monitors", pupils who had already learned the lesson, and in turn, taught it to the other pupils.   The favorable public reception of Lancaster's method was due, in part, to his discovery of a cost effective way to increase instruction to the poor. The use of this system stimulated financial help from people of wealth and even contributions from the royal family.[32]

A different kind of educational provision came from the

London Infant School Society. This organization was founded to further the education of children "at one year or as soon as they could walk" to age six.[33] Robert Owen was the motivational force behind this movement and used it to promulgate some of his basic beliefs. Owen held that the circumstances of the environment, especially in early life, molded one's character. To this end, Owen and the London Infant School Society presumed that the sooner a child began learning in the proper setting, the stronger his character would be.

The infant school movement met with objection. The schools, described as "galleries of babes watching their teacher," were reported to have as many as two hundred children from the ages of two to seven cramped in a single room.[34] Aside from the less than optimal physical conditions, parents thought these schools would weaken the moral ties of the family and would promote socialist ideals. Moreover, parental resentment swelled when the schools showed the children the errors of the parents' way of life. Yet for all the ill feeling which was generated, the infant school furnished a place for the small child to go when his mother, father, and older siblings were at work in the factories. Furthermore, the schools did impart a little reading and a few manual skills, such as sewing, even if in a confined and ill-ventilated atmosphere. In truth, the environment in the school was similar to the environment of the child at home. Yet an added advantage to the school surroundings was that they usually contained a secure playground, which greatly reduced the number of street urchins wandering mischieviously about town.

Jeremy Bentham and James Mill were both in agreement with their contemporaries who stressed the influence of the environment on a child's education. Together they collaborated on the education of John Stuart Mill, James' eldest son. Bentham's works were endlessly filled with grandiose schemes. He envisioned elaborate educational institutions controlling the entire learning environment for maximum student benefit. James Mill, who reasoned on a smaller scale than Bentham, emphasized the educational opportunities which naturally occurred during an individual's lifetime. However, both Bentham and Mill wrote that much of a man's true education came outside of the formal school environment. With the earlier classicals, T. R. Malthus and David Ricardo, they shared a limited view of educational finance: they judged that philanthropic efforts would be sufficient to meet the educational needs of the common man.

To some extent religious contributions and private philanthropy had succeeded in providing popular education in England. Since the basic need had been met by independent means, state involvement in education was not occasioned by a call for essential

8

instruction. It was begun indirectly through the need for state interference in the work place. The first legislation to deal with education was the Factory Act, or the Health and Morals of Apprentices Act of 1802.[35] This law limited the hours of work for apprentices in the cotton and woolen mills to twelve a day and specified that some part of the apprentice's work day be set aside for elementary instruction. A broader Factory Act was passed in 1833. This act prohibited the employment of all children under the age of nine and also required the attendance at school of all children between the ages of nine and thirteen for two hours a day. To assure adequate facilities to carry out this legislation, a grant of twenty thousand pounds was voted by Parliament "in aid of public subscription for the erection of school-houses for the education of children of the poorer classes in Great Britain."[36] Essentially, these first monies were divided between the National Society and the British and Foreign Schools Society. Nevertheless, other groups starting schools also were able to receive aid for their buildings under this grant.[37] This 1833 act marked the beginning of state involvement in British education.

Growth of the state in education necessitated administrative machinery to supervise the activity. First, a special committee of the Privy Council was established in 1839 to administer the government grants and for "the consideration of all matters affecting the education of the people."[38] The Education Department of the Privy Council was the successor to the original committee and supervised the changes affected by the passage of the Elementary Education Act in 1870.[39] This act empowered the government itself to furnish educational facilities for the first time. Moreover, under the 1870 legislation, popularly elected school boards would be organized to superintend schools for pupils between the ages of five and thirteen in areas where no voluntary schools existed or where the supply of elementary education was judged inadequate.[40] By the end of the century the British government had become a visible participant in the educational system.

John Stuart Mill, John McCulloch, and Nassau W. Senior all witnessed the gradual involvement of the English government in society, especially in the educational field. Each man played a part in the emerging social consciousness of late Victorian England. To them the social and economic plight of the working child was too serious to ignore. Child labor had been shown to be the cause of more than personal temporary distress. Over the century, its long run societal disadvantages had also become readily apparent. All three economists viewed the legislative changes in support of a more humanitarian social structure as essential to societal well-being. Yet, each economist realized the dangerous possibilities in these new socio-economic rules.

9

The final pieces of legislation committing England to state supported universal education began to fall into place in 1876 when elementary education was made compulsory to age ten.[41] Next in 1891, a law was passed to provide education free of charge to pupils in state aided elementary schools. To defray the costs of this program, the state guaranteed grants to the schools to compensate them for the loss of student fees.[42] Finally, in 1899, school attendance to age twelve was legislated.

Henry Sidgwick and Henry Fawcett wrote of the educational system in Britain as it was being cemented together over the century. Fawcett was not pleased with the construction; only in very specific circumstances did he believe it would stand. Sidgwick, on the other hand, examined the foundation of the scheme. He found that an educational system built around state interference rested on firm logical economic reasoning. He thought the rationale for state provision had been well constructed.

Herbert Spencer examined the English state educational edifice once it was in place. He was repelled by the social and economic philosophers who could accept so radical a change in the social fabric of a nation without seeing the obvious dangers of such change. Spencer recalled the arguments of his predecessors who had written before the rise of government power in education. He hoped the ideas of the earlier thinkers whose minds had not been sullied by the omnipresence of government could be used to awaken contemporary social policy makers to the alternatives that were still available under a free market educational system. Spencer single-handedly crusaded against the growing popular sentiment.

THE CLASSICAL POLITICAL ECONOMISTS AND EDUCATIONAL POLICY

Gradually, the people of Europe adopted the concept of state provision of universal basic education. A century had elapsed before the final changes were in place. Slowly European political and economic thinkers came to accept state involvement as a possible solution to the problems of the day. When they did, government interference in education was assured. This book examines the educational thoughts of some European economic philosophers, who were writing during the formation of the educational policy of their countries.

Economists, as other social scientists, endeavor to explain the phenomena which they observe using the tools which they know best. Since the earliest classical economists were moral philosophers, their basic ideas on education were philosophical.

10

However, since they were also economists, they easily delved into practical political-economic solutions to educational problems. On balance, their educational philosophy is a poor second to their economic analysis of education. The political economists were on firm ground when they examined the macroeconomic and microeconomic effects of education. All of the writers studied in this book observed the benefits which education could give society as a whole. Some of the classical authors referred to the macroeconomic benefits of all types of education; others concentrated on the nation-wide good that would result from universally provided basic education. Moreover, the classical authors contended that the microeconomic effects of education could be easily observed in the changes which occurred in an individual's life. The most conspicuous microeconomic result was an increase in the individual's wage. However, there were other microeconomic benefits, such as the increase in personal health and happiness which upgraded the individual's self-esteem and which might mean almost as much to him as additional income. The macroeconomic and microeconomic examination of educational provision by the classical political economists was quite thorough.

The majority of the classical economists acknowledged the fact that the service, education, was unlike other services and required special analytical treatment. Education did not fit into the established reasoning of classical economic theory which relied on the free market for the supply of and demand for goods and services. Special analytical tools had to be developed to deal with the complex problem of educational provision.

New tools of economic analysis were employed as they were being explored; the problem of education would not wait long for a solution. The economists did much of their thinking even while the educational laws were being written. Altering their traditional ways of thinking was not easy for these men. Even though they firmly believed in the good that education could yield for the masses, the determination of educational providers was a very thorny issue. They hesitated to prescribe government involvement too hastily.

Decision making for each economic writer revolved around several crucial points of reasoning. First, the economist had to reason that universal education was a socially desirable good which would not be provided in adequate amounts by the private sector. If this line of thought were adopted, then a new class of goods and services had to be identified, a class where goods were supplied more efficiently by the state rather than by individuals. There was a split in classical reasoning at this point. Some classical thinkers did not agree that universal education was socially desirable to the extent that the free market system of supply should be significantly altered. Others accepted basic

11

education as a social good but suggested a variety of schemes which involved as many free market principles as possible. Still others felt that universal education was so important to social welfare that the free market could rightly be ignored if ignoring it would expedite the flow of basic knowledge to the common people.

Furthermore, since most of the classical political economists were trained as political philosophers, the ideas of rights and freedom in society were important to them. Throughout many of their writings there exists the thread of a discussion about the educational rights of children and the corresponding duties of parents. These ideas spill over into thoughts regarding the rights of parents to rely on their children's incomes for family support. The problem of the opportunity cost of a child's labor when it was required for family sustenance led many policy makers to suggest compulsory education laws as the only certain way to ensure universal schooling. This suggestion struck squarely at the heart of individual liberty. As free market economists, many of these authors had to make intellectual concessions to allow public goods to be provided by the state; as champions of liberty, these political thinkers had to find a justification for a basic infringement on freedom.

THE AUTHORS

The authors covered in this book are political economists or political philosophers most of whom wrote during the nineteenth century. They run the gamut from the most well-known economist of all, Adam Smith, to some who would be called "economists" only in relation to their educational ideas, such as Wilhelm von Humboldt and Herbert Spencer. Some examined education thoroughly in all of its facets (Smith, again); others mentioned education in passing, almost as a subject not worthy of much extensive consideration (Ricardo, for example). Each writer was chosen for this work because of his individualized contribution to the total thought of the classicals on education.

Adam Smith (1723 - 1790) was selected for this book because he introduced such a broad spectrum of economic ideas to the world at large in his seminal works. Education was not overlooked in his comprehensive economic thought. Jeremy Bentham (1748 - 1832) presented unique educational plans which were typical of the projects of his contemporaries. Bentham and his friend, James Mill, actively attempted to have their educational ideas put into practice and sought to make personal and monetary gains from their education related endeavors. Wilhelm von Humboldt (1767 - 1835), more a political philosopher than a political economist, was responsible for a major revision of the Prussian educational system. Nevertheless, his personal thoughts on the benefits of education and the role of the state in education are surprisingly candid for one who served as the Minister of Worship and Public Instruction for his country.

T. R. Malthus (1766 - 1834) and David Ricardo (1772 - 1823) were traditional classical political economists. They viewed education as tangential to their main thrust but were well aware of its power to change men. Jean Baptiste Say (1767 - 1832) presented the Frenchman's view of universal education before the French Revolution. He optimistically envisioned an enlightened citizenry under the tutelage of the state. Say's ideas were quite different from those of the characteristic turn of the century Englishmen, like James Mill. Mill (1773 - 1836), a strong advocate of the powers of education to affect societal change, served as the spokesman for the British educational thinking of his day when he wrote the entry on "Education" for the 1818 *Encyclopaedia Britannica*.

J. R. McCulloch (1789 - 1864) and Nassau Senior (1790 - 1864) were influenced by the sordid conditions which they observed in the factory districts throughout England. McCulloch and Senior both suggested using the best parts of the existing educational structure as a foundation for a workable plan for future instruction. John Stuart Mill (1806 - 1873), the eclectic, offered an expanded version of prior political economic thought on education. This he embellished with some novel ideas of his own.

Claude Frederic Bastiat (1801 - 1850) perceived the effects of French state involvement in education after the take-over of Napoleon. Englishman, Herbert Spencer (1820 - 1903) denounced the strong involvement of his government in education as the nineteenth century came to a close. Bastiat and Spencer recorded opinions which were contrary to those of most of their contemporaries. Many of the other classical writers acknowledged the importance of the free market in their educational thought but gradually accepted government in education as somehow inevitable. Bastiat and Spencer both feared the widespread adoption of the idea of government provision of "necessary" goods and services. They foresaw that this was the start of a new political-economic system, one in which the government played an increasingly dominant role.

Karl Marx (1818 - 1883) and Friedrich Engles (1820 - 1895) looked forward to a new social order. In their writings education played a powerful part in bringing about the desired societal change. Marx and Engles were very definite about the kind of education that should be furnished for the future society: they demanded education devoid of bourgeois control. Only through this kind of instruction could the workers of the nation rise to meet their potential.

The final two economists studied in this book are Henry Fawcett (1833 - 1884) and Henry Sidgwick (1938 - 1900). Each gave a different summary of the classical position on education. Fawcett offered little in terms of a comprehensive analysis of the macroeconomic aspects of the education problem, but he did introduce a microeconomic consideration which was in keeping with the subsequent wave of analysis on income elasticity. Sidgwick, on the other hand, provided a thoroughly modern explanation of the reasons why government might become involved in the educational process. Sidgwick took the classical arguments and formalized and renovated them. He then introduced these reworked classical concepts into what eventually became the common body of neo-classical economic thinking about the place of education within the socio-economic system.

The writings of these authors were examined first for their educational philosophy, such as it was. Then each writer's work was perused for his ideas on the macroeconomic and microeconomic effects of education on the society. The groundwork laid in the examination of these concepts provided the classical writers with a basic framework for their analyses of the demand for and the supply of education.

Working from the foundation established in their demand and supply theory, many of the classical economic writers presented an educational plan or part of an educational plan for the dissemination of universal knowledge. These plans were diverse, running from an amended free market approach to total government control. In these plans the author often presented his opinion of the state's role in education. These opinions, too, were as different as the men who held them.

One obvious fact that emerged from the study of the educational thought of the classical political economists was that the thinking of each of these writers was in many respects significantly different from that of his contemporaries. Thus, it would be futile to try to present a single dogmatic classical economic analysis of educational provision. In keeping with this idea, the bulk of this book records the variety apparent in the educational thinking of the classicists. Nevertheless, similarities in the thinking of these writers do surface, especially in a comparison with contemporary ideas on the economics of education. Therefore, the last chapter of the book examines the influence of the general body of classical educational thought on the political economic thinking of today.

NOTES

1. See, for example: Kirk Willis, "The Role in Parliament of the Economic Ideas of Adam Smith, 1776-1800," , Vol. 11 (2), pp. 503-544.

2. William Boyd and Edmund J. King, *The History of Western Education*, 10th ed. (New York, 1973), p. 280.

3. J. H. Higginson in "Dame Schools" in the *British Journal of Educational Studies* described the goal of these schools as to teach the pupils "their letters and keep them out of harm's way," Vol. 22 (2), p. 168.

4. The "hedge" school is another example of the dubious quality of the education that was provided for children during this period. It got its name from the fact that the instructors were so "irregular" that they had to hold their schools behind a hedge or some similar apparatus to shield them from public view.

5. Secondary schools were called "grammar schools" for the Latin grammar which was taught there.

6. Luella Cole, *A History of Education* (New York, 1955),p. 440.

7. Reference Division of the British Information Service, *Education in Britain* (New York, 1966), p. 3.

8. In early 1700, John Locke had commented on the state of these institutions: "Why ... does the learning of Latin and Greek need the rod ...? Children learn to dance and fence without whipping ...: which would make one suspect that there is something strange, unnatural and disagreeable to that age, in the things required in grammar schools or in the methods used there, that children cannot be brought to without the severity of the lash, and hardly with that too." Boyd and King, p. 275.

9. See: Theodore Zeldin, "Higher Education in France, 1848 - 1940", *The Journal of Contemporary History*, Vol. 2 (3). pp. 53-80.

10. *Education in Britain*, p. 59.

11. Ibid.

15

12. Ibid.

13. James Mulhern, *A History of Education* (New York, 1946), p. 432.

14. Francisco Cordasco, *A Brief History of Education* (Totowa, N.J., 1970), p. 95.

15. See: "Higher Education in Germany in the Nineteenth Century" by Fritz Ringer in *The Journal of Contemporary History*, Vol. 2 (3), pp. 123-138, especially p. 128.

16. Ibid.

17. Boyd and King, p. 283.

18. See: Carla Thomas' "Philosophical Anthropology and Educational Change: Wilhelm von Humboldt and the Prussian Reforms," *History of Education Quarterly*, Vol. 13 (3), pp. 219-229.

19. Boyd and King, p. 284. For an expansion of the thesis that Rousseau's ideas are the heart of modern progressive education see: Elijahu Rosenow, "Rousseau's 'Emile', An Anti-Utopia" in the *British Journal of Educational Studies*, Vol. 27 (3). pp. 212-224.

20. Boyd and King, p. 305.

21. French Cultural Services, *The French System of Education* (New York, undated), p. 2.

22. Mulhern, p. 442.

23. Boyd and King, p. 360.

24. *French System of Education*, pp. 1-2.

25. See: Raymond Grew, Patrick Harrigan, with James Whitney, "The Availability of Schooling in Nineteenth Century France," *Journal of Interdisciplinary History*, Vol. 14 (1), pp. 25-63.

26. War, once again, had figured prominently in the promotion of education. After the Franco-Prussian War, the occupation of large parts of French territory by Prussian troops, coupled with many stories of battles lost through the ignorance of French soldiers, led the French press to exclaim: "The Prussian teacher has won the war;" see: W. Van Vliet and J. A. Smyth, "A Nineteenth-Century Proposal to Use School

Vouchers," *Comparative Education Review*, Vol. 26 (1), p. 96.

27. Boyd and King, p. 282.

28. Cordasco, p. 87, and W. H. G. Armytage, *Four Hundred Years of English Education* (Cambridge, 1970), p. 41.

29. Boyd and King, p. 282; it is interesting that a preclassical economist, Bernard Mandeville, presented a criticism of charity schools in his 1723 tale, *The Fable of the Bees: or, Private Vices; Public Benefits*. This work was originally published in 1714 as an *Essay on Charity and Charity Schools* and a *Search into the Nature of Society*; see: Armytage, pp. 46-47.

30. Armytage, pp. 90-92; the full name of this second educational group was the Institution for Promoting the British System for the Education of the Labouring and Manufacturing Classes of Every Religious Persuasion.

31. Dr. Bell (1753-1832), a Scotsman, had independently discovered the monitorial method at the same time as Lancaster. The National Society supported Dr. Bell's system since it included doctrine of the established church. Dissenters followed the "Lancasterian method."

32. Boyd and King. p. 306.

33. Cordasco, p. 88.

34. See: A. F. B. Roberts, "A New View of the Infant School Movement," *British Journal of Educational Studies*, Vol. 20 (2), pp. 154-164.

35. Boyd and King, p. 368.

36. Ibid., p. 369.

37. *Education in Britain*, p. 4.

38. Boyd and King, p. 369.

39. It is significant that this important piece of educational legislation was passed just three years after the vote had been given to the working class people of the town.

40. This resulted in a dual system of grant-aided elementary schools, one supplied by the churches and other voluntary

bodies and the other supplied by the state through school boards.

41. Mulhern, p. 453.

42. In Britain, all except the very poor paid small fees for elementary education until 1891.

CHAPTER II

THE EDUCATIONAL PHILOSOPHY OF THE
CLASSICAL POLITICAL ECONOMISTS

The early classical political economists were moral philosophers. As such, they concentrated on a variety of disci-
plines, for example, philosophy, theology, jurisprudence, and
political economy. These men examined the rationale behind
popular economic and social theories as well as examining the
theories themselves. The basis for much of their reasoning was
the natural law since eighteenth and nineteenth century thought
in both the natural and moral sciences was steeped in the natural
law tradition. Simply stated, these thinkers sought the "natural"
solution to a physical or a moral problem.

The natural law philosophy of the classical political
economists' education theory was best observed in their dedication
to domestic education. The economists preferred nature's method
of rearing the young through close parental association. All this
parent-child relationship needed was direction and it would result
in the best educational experience possible. Monitoring this
education would have to be complete since all aspects of the environment which surrounded the learning experience were important. For instance, if the child were trying to learn the lessons
of life at his mother's knee while she was begging for bread in
the street, the child's education would surely incorporate his
squalid surroundings. The classicals considered the instruction
which a child received from the earliest experiences through
young adulthood as essential to the formation of his character.
Of all the influences which affected that character, parental
concern and physical surroundings were considered by all of the
writers to be very significant.

Adam Smith found "natural harmony" in domestic education.
The foundation of Smith's natural law philosophy of education was
parental love. The love of parents for their children was so
strong, Smith remarked, that "in the Decalogue we are commanded
to honor our fathers and mothers. No mention is made of the
love of our children."[1] Smith continued by pointing out that the
love of parents for their offspring was a necessary part of the
human cycle because human children were dependent upon their
parents for so long a period of time. This dependence both allowed and necessitated the education of children in the domestic
environment, he believed. Smith wrote: "We may observe an utility in this constitution of our nature that children have so long a
dependence upon their parents, to bring down their passions to
theirs, and thus be trained up at length to become useful members of society."[2] Smith felt that nature furnished the keys to

the continued existence of society through domestic training of the young. His strong feelings on this point were obvious when he set down: "Every child gets this piece of education, even under the most worthless parent."[3]

Smith commented on the common practice of sending children away from home to distant "public" boarding schools and nunneries. This act was against the philosophy of educating under "natural" circumstances, and Smith was not surprised that undesired results were often obtained. He wondered how parents could expect their children to return home filled with filial piety and sibling affection when these children had been deprived of the domestic environment which nurtured these very sentiments. In his best natural law fashion, Smith concluded this part of his discussion on education with: "Domestic education is the institution of nature; public education, the contrivance of man. It is surely unnecessary to say which is likely to be the wisest."[4]

James Mill, as Smith, held that natural surroundings provided much of the true education of society. Mill, however, went beyond Smith's analysis of the benefits received from education obtained in the home and included in his work a discussion of the training received on the job, the knowledge acquired from interaction with other men, and the insights attained from government involvement in the life of each individual. Mill identified four types of education, each of which described one area of learning in the child-student environment.

The first kind of education in Mill's educational quartet was Domestic education. This included "all that the child hears and sees; more especially, all that it is made to suffer or enjoy at the hands of others."[5] Mill, as Smith, placed great faith in the strength of parental influence. Even accounting for "defective" parents, he believed that "no other source of generosity in Human Nature produces uniformly so large a portion of its proper effects."[6]

Technical training was Mill's second kind of education. This was concerned with training the intellect. Through technical education, men were taught the skills to perform the various tasks necessary in life. Moreover, Mill maintained that each person should bear the responsibility of his own technical training. Since the ultimate reason behind education in a particular skill was an increase in personal productivity, Mill assumed that the market and individuals themselves would be the best judges of the types of vocational instruction needed in society.

In the case of the third type of education, Social education, society was the educator and the student learned through imitation and through the circumstances of "happiness and misery" in which society placed him. Mill saw association spillovers from this type of social instruction: "With the idea of our own acts of virtue there are naturally associated the ideas of all the immense advantages we derive from the virtuous acts of our Fellow-creatures. When this association is formed in due strength, which it is the main business of a good education to effect, the motive of virtue becomes paramount in the human breast."[7] Mill believed that social education went beyond concern for the individual alone and affected the education of the entire group.

Finally, Political education was the keystone of Mill's educational arch. Mill was awed by "the political machine (which) acts immediately upon the mind and with extraordinary power." As omnipresent as the direct effects of government were, the indirect effects were equally overwhelming to Mill as he remarked, "(government) acts upon almost everything else by which the character of the mind is apt to be formed."[8] The power of government in the environment was an educational force which could not be ignored Mill perceived. By including Political education, Mill had completed his description of the domestic, technical, social and political influences through which the student was molded into an adult by the educational opportunities existing in his environment.

James Mill believed so strongly in the role of the environment in education that he was willing to use the education of his eldest son to illustrate the beneficial results of a highly controlled educational experience. Mill personally educated his son, John Stuart, in a closely monitored physical environment and with a curriculum wholly determined by James Mill himself. By this experiment he hoped to prove the validity of the newly discovered psychological Principle of Association which stressed the enormous power of the environment on a child's character.[9]

In conducting this experiment, Mill's aim was true. His fundamental contention was that a child was educated to render him "as much as possible, an instrument of happiness, first to himself, and next to other beings."[10] He thought that to achieve this goal, strong direction, bordering on mental conditioning, was needed. Mill's thoughts are unambiguous in these words: "As the happiness, which is the end of education, depends upon the actions of the individual, and as all the actions of man are produced by his feelings or thoughts, the business of education is to make certain feelings or thoughts take place instead of others. The business of education, then, is to work upon the mental successions."[11] James Mill thought that he could inculcate into John Stuart all of the knowledge and information that was necessary to make him a happy and productive citizen.

In this task, Mill called upon his personal friend and

intellectual companion, Jeremy Bentham who shared a common philosophy with Mill. Mill was an ardent follower of Bentham's utilitarian philosophical beliefs which were based on the analysis of the pleasures and pains in human actions. He considered pleasure and pain the result of natural laws and he felt that the task of education was to teach individuals what these natural laws were. Mill identified an erroneous association between pleasure and pain which was due to "bad Education; and is highly unfortunate; for the value of the pleasures in question is infinitely outweighed by the value of the pains. The business of a good education is to make the associations and values correspond."[12] In essence, Mill combined utilitarian philosophy with the psychological principle of association in the fundamental principles of his educational philosophy.

Although Mill believed that natural elements of education were furnished in the home and the work place, as well as through social and political intercourse, he did not hold that education should be abandoned to chance. If the conditions of the environment were well ordered, he reasoned, the education which was produced in the society would be in keeping with right social values. Furthermore, Mill was convinced that education which resulted from "bad" elements in society was "bad" education and should be eradicated by societal change.

John Stuart Mill's education might be the best proof of the efficacy of his father's educational ideas. John Stuart was educated to be the worthy successor of Mill and Bentham and was given the "right experiences for shaping the mind" in Bentham's very garden. A well-known record of the outcome of this experiment exists in John Stuart Mill's *Autobiography*.[13] In this book he documented his reactions to a controlled educational environment, recollecting the pains and pleasures of his youth from the vantage point of adulthood.

Much of Mill's instruction was directed toward producing the perfect Benthamite. John Stuart was especially proud of the training he had received in utilitarian logic and in the detection of fallacy.[14] In the *Autobiography*, Mill described his father's method for teaching him how to reason: "(He) strove to make the understanding not only go along with every step of the teaching, but, if possible, precede it. Any theory which could be found out by thinking I was never told, until I had exhausted my efforts to find it out for myself."[15] However, there were drawbacks to a steady diet of "logic and analysis" and Mill felt that his emotional and aesthetic development had been surpressed. He reported wanly that his education had lacked "poetic culture."[16]

In generalizing about his education, John Stuart used the words "unusual" and "remarkable". More directly, he claimed that it was in striking contrast to what he thought was the essentially "wasted" effort of contemporary instruction. Mill recalled that "cram" was never allowed as a method of study; he recorded that he had never engaged in the exercise of committing "learning" to memory. In a letter to Carlyle, Mill set down the long run benefits of learning without memorizing as he wrote: "Fortunately however I was not crammed; my own thinking faculties were called into strong though partial play; and by their means I have been enabled to *remake* all my opinions."[17] It was interesting to note that at least some of James Mill's teaching methodology was judged worthwhile by his singular pupil.

The "partial" development of John Stuart's faculties became very obvious to him when his education was complete and he was forced into a world of people who were not recipients of the Bentham-Mill method of education. At this point he realized that he had been robbed of natural boyhood experiences in his father's determination to shelter him from the corrupting influence of other boys. One modern author has observed about this relation: "The father who wanted to immunize his son against the contagion of vulgar modes of thought and feeling left the son vulnerable to psychological infection, contracted from too early and enervating an exposure to the rarefied atmosphere of mind."[18] His father's overprotection had left John Stuart feeling psychologically inferior to his peers. This impression of incompleteness eventually drove Mill to a severly depressed state as a young adult. Mill claimed that his condition was finally alleviated by making up his deficiency in "poetic culture" reading poetry, especially Wordsworth. Since Mill believed that poetry had been the source of personal salvation when all other forms of mental exercise had failed him, he became a strong advocate for the inclusion of the subject into the higher education curriculum.

There were other aspects of John Stuart Mill's personal education which influenced his thought on social education. He had first hand knowledge of the Lancaster monitorial teaching method which was being touted by some (including Bentham and James Mill) as the cheapest and most efficient way to teach.[19] John Stuart was responsible for putting this method into practice when, attending his father's instructions, he taught his younger siblings what he himself had only recently learned. He completely disliked this way of teaching although he admitted that personally he had "learned more thoroughly and retained more lastingly the things which I was set to teach."[20] Nevertheless, he was not convinced of the benefits of the monitorial method of teaching for his students. Second, when James Mill penned the *Elements of Political Economy* in 1821, a reworking of Ricardian economic thought for beginners, he used John Stuart as an intermediary. The writing followed this pattern: James gave his son a lesson on political economy; John Stuart wrote the lesson down, rewriting it until the notes were perfectly clear; reviewing John's notes, James constructed his book around them. In another of James Mill's literary endeavors, the *History of British India*, completed in 1818, John Stuart read the manuscript while his father read the proofs. In both of these early exercises, John Stuart was being trained to rewrite the thoughts of another rather than to create original ideas. The emphasis on synthesizing past writers was obvious in Mill's thoughts on education. Much of what Mill had to contribute to educational thought had been analyzed by classical writers before him.

Mill himself realized his propensity to arrange rather than initiate in a parallel context when he observed that he had no preparation in manual skills. He wrote that his education was "more fitted for training me to *know* than to *do*."[21] This lack of hands-on training bothered Mill so much that he warned his readers: "books and schooling are absolutely necessary to education; but not all sufficient."[22] Mill went on to specify the "first principle" of intellectual development as "that in which the mind is active, not that in which it is passive."[23] In his own instruction, Mill sensed that his education had been overloaded with abstract knowledge, but it was deficient in clues as to its use.

The most positive attribute that John Stuart ascribed to his individualized education was that it gave him the "advantage of a quarter of a century over my contemporaries."[24] This advantage did not cause him to have feelings of gratitude towards his father, however. In fact, James Mill was generally regarded as a fearful tyrant by all of his offspring.[25] In reflecting upon his father's teaching methods, John Stuart penned a revealing comment in his *Autobiography* when he wrote, "As regards my own education, I hesitate to pronounce whether I was more a loser or a gainer by his severity."[26]

Even if John Stuart did not hold to his father's educational methodology, he did concur with his educational philosophy in many respects. The younger Mill strongly agreed with his father on three key concepts regarding education: (1) the heart of education was mental enrichment, (2) the power of education to affect society was tremendous, and (3) the environment played a crucial role in the making of an individual's character. First, John Stuart perceived that "the end of education is not to teach, but to fit the mind for learning from its own consciousness and observation."[27] He also recognized the power of education to overcome natural weaknesses: "the power of education is almost boundless: there is not one natural inclination which it is not strong enough to coerce, and, if needful, destroy ... ."[28] Finally, John Stuart wrote of the role of the environment on the individual and of the ability of education to cause changes within that environment: "differences in education and outward circumstances are capable of affording an adequate explanation of by far the greatest portion of character ... ."[29]

The similarities with James Mill's educational ideas notwithstanding, John Stuart Mill was especially conscious of the need for intellectual development within a free and unstructured atmosphere, an atmosphere diametrically opposed to that of his youthful training. In his pursuit of an unfettered opportunity for the development of the young, he was strongly influenced by Wilhelm von Humboldt whom he quoted in the opening words of *On Liberty*. Mill, as Humboldt, visualized "human nature (not as) a machine to be built after a model, and set to do exactly the work prescribed for it, but a tree, which requires to grow and develop itself on all sides, according to the tendency of the inward forces which make it a living thing."[30] Mill judged that the type of education which existed within a society could enhance or destroy the diversity in human nature, a concept often expressed in Humboldt's writings. As Mill recorded: "All that has been said of the importance of the individuality of character, and the diversity in opinions and modes of conduct, involves, as of the same unspeakable importance, diversity of education."[31]

In their love for the uniqueness of the individual, Humboldt and John Stuart Mill held many similar educational ideas. Humboldt supported the notion that it was the singular elements among men that were worth expanding through education. From this he reasoned that self knowledge was the goal of any education. He considered, "it is only our own self that we may ... learn to know and to let such knowledge bear fruit in us."[32] Like James and John Stuart Mill, he admitted that external institutions could stimulate learning by strengthening the individual's natural capabilities and inclinations. However, Humboldt was firm in his conviction that true education came from within.

Additionally, Humboldt thought that mistakenly applied education was a social waste, an opinion shared by James Mill. Yet, like John Stuart Mill, he viewed the individual's individuality as a precious quality which would be crushed by the weight of a structured learning experience. Humboldt reflected that since children in the developmental years do not display the fullness of their unique talents, harm might result from imposing strong external constraints on their intellectual growth. He recorded that "it is downright dangerous to fail to appreciate those who are only on their way toward full development. That is why it is so necessary, but also so difficult for an educator to recognize true individuality."[33]

Humboldt spent much time considering education and the role of the state in education since he was the director of the Prussian education system in his official position as Minister of

Worship and Public Instruction. Even though he achieved large strides for public education in his state, he felt inadequate in this occupation. He confided to his wife, "I have no skill whatever at educating ... . I have never had any real love for it. To be an educator at any level (and even the Minister of Public Instruction is an educator, if he is right for his job) one needs a certain pedantic, complacent credulity as to the good results to be had from education."[34] Humboldt felt that he did not possess the required faith in the power of a formal education system to do all that its proponents claimed for it. Ironically, he often returned to the thought that much formal education was fruitless: "Important as the influence of education may be on the course of a man's life, the hereditary and environmental conditions which accompany him throughout his life are far more so. Where these forces do not work hand in hand, education alone can make no dent whatever."[35]

Heredity and environment were significant in determining a child's intellectual development, but parental input determined both heredity and environment, Humboldt, as Smith and James Mill believed. He expressed his sentiments in very strong terms. If the choice were between parental influence in education and state influence in education, Humboldt could answer clearly: "If it only intended to prevent the possibility of children remaining uninstructed, it is much more convenient and less harmful to appoint guardians where parents are remiss, or to subsidize them when they are indigent."[36] Notably, Humboldt, who had helped to create a state educational system which was the envy of Europe, still placed education in the home as the most important and basic of all instruction.

As much as Humboldt and the Mills prized education born of natural influences, Karl Marx and Friedrich Engles disfavored it. This classical duo was critical of domestic education in which parents educated their own offspring. Marx maintained that parental education resulted in educators being selected by "mere accidents of birth," and "entails a partiality which stands in the way of a good education."[37] The inevitable result of this educational inbreeding would be to prolong the evils inherent in the status quo. Marx disliked the natural educational relationship and he disliked the subjects that were naturally associated with it. He expressed disbelief at the English bourgeoisie which attempted to teach workers the "natural laws of commerce." Marx regarded the bourgeoisie as "childish" and "silly" since they could not see that these very "natural" laws necessarily "lead (the worker) to pauperism."[38]

Both Marx and Engles were keenly aware of the power of parental education to create and sustain class differences. Marx supposed that "this ... must divide society into two parts - one

26

which towers above."[39] They had confidence in the fact that these class differences would result in an eventual disruption of the social order. Contemporary education, Marx noted, could be "comprehended and rationally understood only as 'revolutionary practice.'"[40] Marx suggested that "education itself was in need of a good education."[41] And Engles warned the bourgeoisie of the disastrous consequences which occurred in a fragmented, class conscious society left to follow its "natural" inclinations. His words went unheeded and, he recorded, " ... in England, for three hundred years, the educated and all the learned people have been deaf and blind to the signs of the times."[42]

Engles had been studying the signs of the times in Britain, especially in the 1840's. His first work of international repute was *The Condition of the Working Class in England* in which he examined compliance with the education legislation then in existence. He observed that state examiners were appalled at the conditions they found; the children knew neither how to read nor how to write. The education which the working children *did* receive was in the harsh realities of life in the factories. Engles commented that the workers would be awakened by this "practical training" to the knowledge of "where his own interest and that of the nation lies." As class differences were sharpened by the brutal education of factory life, the worker would gradually learn "what the especial interest of the bourgeoisie is, and what he has to expect of that bourgeoisie."[43] Engles questioned the wisdom of the bourgeoisie who would not even impart to the workers the *moral* doctrines of the middle class. He decided that the possibility of using education to perpetuate the capitalistic order was totally disregarded by those who had the most to lose from its demise.

In contrast to Marx and Engles who envisioned education as a divisive force in a capitalistic society, Herbert Spencer believed that free market education could be a unifying element in a free market society. Spencer's associations with education were lifelong. He was a descendant of a long line of teachers and, similar to John Stuart Mill's experience, his father and uncle personally supervised young Herbert's education. In 1861 Spencer received widespread attention for a small book containing four essays entitled *Education: Intellectual, Moral, and Physical*. In this book he systematized his father's educational methodology of stressing three points: (1) sympathy over authority, (2) instruction individualized to the level of the student, and (3) use of practical examples whenever possible.[44]

This work also introduced two of Spencer's basic ideas on education. First, he examined the nature of education, describing the "unfolding of a child's mind ... like the unfolding of the mind of the human race. Education must proceed from the simple

27

to the more complex; self development should be encouraged to the uttermost in the child."[45] Throughout his writings, Spencer emphasized this idea stressing that "society is a product of development and not of manufacture."[46] Second, he reiterated the pivotal place of each individual in his own training and, correspondingly, the detrimental effects that interlopers could have: "The vital knowledge – that by which we have grown as a nation to what we are and which underlies our whole existence, is a knowledge that has got itself taught in nooks and corners: while the ordained agencies for teaching have been mumbling little else than dead formulas."[47]

Spencer pursued these concepts in subsequent works. He questioned even the need for formalized instruction, appealing to basic principles which existed in nature to make his case. He called to mind that nature adequately took care of the plants and animals; why, then, he wondered, was it that the human mind alone tended to develop itself incorrectly? Spencer did admit that education could be used without doubt in one rare circumstance, to teach savages social graces; but he concluded that even this would be short lived since "like other institutions resulting from the non-adaptation of man to the social state, (this form of education) must in the end die out."[48] Furthermore, knowing the advances in universal knowledge which had occurred during his lifetime, Spencer was outraged at the contemporary perception that man was on the verge of perdition because of his lack of formal education. His ire was apparent in these remarks: "Anyone not knowing the past, and judging from the statements of those who have been urging on educational organizations, would suppose that strenuous efforts are imperative to save the people from some gulf of demoralization and crime into which ignorance is sweeping them."[49]

Spencer, as the Mills and Smith, was a proponent of an educational philosophy which identified parental concern as the main building block in a system of education. But this system need not be a structured one, he decided. He would easily concur with Humboldt that formal education was far from the universal solution to the problem of maximizing the individual's potential. Nonetheless, Spencer was generally pleased with the progress he noticed in the expansion of the supply of education to all classes since the time of Adam Smith. Marx and Engles, however, were displeased with any educational plan which relied on the position of an individual in his social class. They did agree with Spencer and the other classical thinkers that environment and heredity set a man on his particular path in life, but they did not believe that the predetermined class-hardened social structure in a capitalistic economy was optimal, either on a personal level or on a social level. Although divided on the goals of education and on the best means of furnishing it to the masses, the classicals all

28

considered domestic education, parental influence, and the environment to be predominant features in the training of the young.

AN ATTEMPT AT A SYSTEM OF EDUCATIONAL THINKING: MILL'S ETHOLOGY

One classical thinker, John Stuart Mill, was dissatisfied with the fragmented thinking on education which he detected among the intellectuals of his day. To rectify this deficiency, he proposed the science of Ethology. He discussed this new science in his early book on logic.

In Mill's *System of Logic*, he considered "the Art of Education." Education was treated as a "practice" or art and was described as an application of the principles dealing with the "Sciences of individual man" and the "Sciences of the actions of the collective masses of mankind."[50] Mill's suggested study of Ethology was to be the foundation of the art of education. A system of practical education would be built on ethological principles. Since Mill hoped that the science would develop the ability to predict the tendencies exhibited by different characters in different circumstances, he dubbed Ethology "the science of character." With this information, education could be tailored to produce the desired results on the individual's character – something that had been the focus of classical economic attention from the earliest times. Since ethological laws described the kind of character produced under all sets of circumstances, both physical and moral, education would include instruction in all of the elements which affected the individual and the societal condition. The application of Ethology, therefore, would have a wide influence on both the nation and on the individual.[51]

Mill was directed towards the invention of the discipline of Ethology because he felt that the objectives of education were not clearly defined. He argued that if schools were institutions established to promote social cohesion, the schools themselves needed a unified foundation upon which to build. Moreover, since any national system of education would be controlled to some degree by social and cultural values, Mill believed that these values should be identified and their effect on individual and national character thoroughly scrutinized.

Although Mill reworked the *System of Logic* through many editions, the section on Ethology was never modified or even developed further. Mill decided that he needed a well conceived system of Psychology upon which to rest his ethological principles. Unfortunately, the psychology of his day was merely an examination of the interaction of ideas. Additional futility plagued early efforts in setting up this science. Alexander Bain, writing *On the Study of Character, Including an Estimate of Phrenology* in 1861, was the first person to attempt to construct an ethological system. Bain freely admitted that his attempt was an unqualified failure.[52] Consequently, Mill's Ethology languished from proper nourishment at the outset and had a dismal introduction to the world at large. But, more importantly, Ethology was considered tangential to the concerns of social scientists in the subsequent decades and was allowed to fade quietly away.

NOTES

1. Adam Smith, *Theory of Moral Sentiments*, eds. D. D. Raphall and A. L. Macfie (Oxford, 1976), p. 142.

2. Adam Smith, *Lectures on Justice, Police, Revenue and Arms*, ed. Edwin Cannan (Oxford, 1896), p. 73.

3. Ibid., p. 74.

4. Smith, *Moral Sentiments*, p. 222.

5. James Mill, *On Education*, ed. W. H. Burston (Cambridge, 1969), p. 52.

6. James Mill, *Analysis of the Phenomena of the Human Mind*, 2nd ed. (New York, 1967), Vol. II, p. 272.

7. Ibid., p. 293.

8. Mill, *On Education*, p. 118.

9. See: "Private versus Public Education, A Classical Economic Dispute" by E. G. West in *The Classical Economists and Economic Policy*, ed. A. W. Coats (London, 1971), and also by the same author, *Education and the Industrial Revolution* (New York, 1975), p. 127. Much of Mill's associationist educational philosophy was summarized in his entry under "Education" for the 1818 *Encyclopaedia Britannica*.

10. Mill, *On Education*, p. 52.

11. Ibid.

12. Mill, *Analysis*, p. 259.

13. John Stuart Mill, *Autobiography of John Stuart Mill* (New York, 1924).

14. Mill himself referred to his early education as "a course in Benthamism," as quoted in *The Improvement of Mankind* by John M. Robson (London, 1968), p. 6.

15. Francis W. Garforth, John Stuart Mill's Theory of Education (New York, 1979), p. 105.

16. John Stuart Mill, *John Stuart Mill on Education*, ed. Francis W. Garforth (New York, 1971), p. 24.

17. Quoted in R. J. Halliday's *John Stuart Mill* (New York, 1976), p. 16.

18. Robert Crossley, "The Failed Educations of John Stuart Mill and Henry Adams, *Journal of General Education*, Vol. 30 (4), p. 243.

19. One recorded criticism of his personal experiment with the monitorial method made by James Mill was in regard to John Stuart's progress in Latin. James said that his son would have progressed more rapidly but that "he is kept back by Billie" (his sister); quoted in "Bentham's 'Chrestomathia': Utilitarian Legacy to English Education," *Journal of the History of Ideas*, Vol. 39 (2), p. 314.

20. Mill, *John Stuart Mill on Education*, p. 48.

21. Ibid., p. 24.

22. John Stuart Mill, *Principles of Political Economy*, ed. William Ashley (Fairfield, 1976), p. 285-7.

23. Ibid., p. 286.

24. Mill, *John Stuart Mill on Education*, p. 24.

25. Edward Alexander, *Matthew Arnold and John Stuart Mill* (New York, 1965), p. 104.

26. Mill, *John Stuart Mill on Education*, p. 83.

27. Garforth, *Theory of Education*, p. 105.

28. John Stuart Mill, *Essays on Ethics, Religion and Society*, ed. J. M. Robson (Toronto, 1969), pp. 408-409.

29. Garforth, *Theory of Education*, p. 53.

30. John Stuart Mill, *On Liberty*, ed. Currin V. Shields (New York, 1956), p. 72.

31. Ibid., p. 129.

32. Wilhem von Humboldt, *Humanist Without Portfolio: An Anthology of the Writings of Wilhelm von Humboldt* (Wayne State University Press, 1963), p. 125.

33. Ibid., p. 131.

34. Ibid., pp. 130–131.

35. Ibid., p. 141.

36. Wilhelm von Humboldt, *The Limits of State Action*, ed. J. W. Burrow (Cambridge, 1969), p. 53.

37. Loyd D. Easton and Kurt H. Guddat, eds. *Writings of the Young Marx on Philosophy and Society* (New York, 1966), p. 103.

38. Ibid., p. 343.

39. Ibid., p. 401.

40. Ibid.

41. Karl Marx and Friedrich Engles, *Collected Works*, (New York, 1975), Vol. I, p. 154.

42. Marx and Engles, *Collected Works*, Vol. III, p. 380.

43. Friedrich Engles, *The Condition of the Working Class in England* (Moscow, 1973), p. 152.

44. See: James G. Kennedy, *Herbert Spencer* (Boston, 1978).

45. David Duncan, *Life and Letters of Herbert Spencer* (New York, 1908), Vol. II, p. 320.

46. Herbert Spencer, *Facts and Comments* (New York, 1902), p. 82.

47. David Wiltshire, *The Social and Political Thought of Herbert Spencer* (Oxford, 1978), p. 7.

48. Herbert Spencer, *Social Statics* (New York, 1954), p. 168.

49. Herbert Spencer, *The Study of Sociology* (Ann Arbor, 1961), p. 71.

50. John Stuart Mill, *On the Logic of the Moral Sciences*, ed. Henry Magid (New York, 1965), p. 46.

51. Ibid.

52. See: "The Fate and Influence of John Stuart Mill's Proposed Science of Ethology" by David E. Leary in the *Journal of the History of Ideas*, Vol. 43 (1), pp. 153-162.

CHAPTER III

THE MACROECONOMICS OF EDUCATION
IN CLASSICAL ECONOMICS

Macroeconomic analysis considers the influences which affect the economy as a whole. This study is in contrast to microeconomics which examines economic events as they affect individual elements within the society. The level of the national product is the prime macroeconomic concern in any economy. Because the amount of national output is determined by the number of individuals employed, the skill of those workers, and the productivity of the tools with which they work, macroeconomists concentrate heavily on national production and its components. An additional type of macroeconomic problem which claimed economists' attention in previous centuries was the "quality" of the laboring classes. This macroeconomic concern for quality was focused only secondarily on work quality; primarily, "moral" quality was at issue as the social responsibility of the lower classes was questioned. The reaction of the workers to their obligation to society affected their daily conduct, both morally and politically. Therefore, it was in the interest of the property holders to support measures which instilled in the working class a sense of social duty while also upgrading their physical productivity. If workers were happily resigned to their circumstances, this contentment would have a positive impact upon the lives of everyone else in the macrosociety.

A special concern of political economists studying the social problems of the time was the problem of how to cope with the changing needs of growing nations in an increasingly competitive world environment. European heads of state constantly engaged one another in military conflict to acquire a more productive piece of land, or a more convenient trade outlet, or even a specific trade concession. The idea that an educated populace could do much to contribute to the solutions of the problems which arose in a complex economic climate was steadily gaining favor. If nothing else, the common people would be able to read enough to be more competent soldiers and so turn the tides of war in favor of the motherland.

The economic wisdom of the mid-eighteenth century called for an advantageous balance in a country's international trading activities. Economists had decided that by raising labor and capital productivity, domestically produced goods could be more competitive abroad and national trade balances could be made more favorable. Increases in product quantity and quality, the classical thinkers reasoned, resulted from the rising skill and educational level of the masses which contributed to technological superiority and greater aggregate output.

Other social economic problems were threatening to under-
mine the established patterns of nineteenth century living. The
social observers of the day were growing alarmed by the presence
of small urchins, "street Arabs," who roamed about the larger
towns engaging in criminal activity. These bands of poor children preyed upon the pockets and consciences of the well-to-do.
Another source of disquietude for the affluent was the ever
present undercurrent of political unrest in the lower classes.
Socially oriented economic philosophy was attracting many of the
uneducated poor. Some industrialists feared that the dangers of
a competing economic system without a private property foundation might be realized if steps were not taken to ameliorate the
conditions of the destitute. Finally, in those charity schools
which did exit, the children might be kept off the streets and
given instruction in good citizenship, but they might also receive
the teaching of some heretical religious sect. The religious poor
man had to face the additional strain of knowing that young minds
were being filled with "erroneous" religious beliefs.

These social interests were closely tied to the macroeconomic
concerns which led the classical political economists to examine
educational provision. Besides their desire to find methods of
increasing a nation's output, the economists also sought ways to
protect individual property rights, and to correct for external
effects. There was little doubt that a literate work force would
yield more products, but is was hoped that other benefits would
occur in the form of popular and universal adherence to the rules
of a system of private property rights. In addition, some anticipated that the literate masses would become companionable with
the rest of society since their learning would expose them to
similar moral and cultural influences.

Adam Smith had no problem identifying respect for law and
order as the highest social good which could be expected from
universal education. The schooled working man had fewer
"delusions of enthusiasm and superstition" and was "more decent
and orderly than an ignorant and stupid one."[1] Smith applauded
education which made the common people "more respectable, and
(therefore) more likely to obtain the respect of their lawful
superiors."[2] These citizens would be "less apt to be misled into
any wanton or unnecessary opposition to the measures of government."[3] Smith felt that the political system itself was threatened
by widespread ignorance in a democratic society: "In free countries where the safety of government depends very much upon
the favorable judgment which the people may form of its conduct,
it must surely be of the highest importance that they should not
be disposed to judge rashly or capriciously concerning it."[4]
Smith had observed the political turmoil which accompanied mass

mistrust of governmental authority. The growing discontent throughout the countryside encouraged him to suggest the dissemination of education as a palliative.

Smith optimistically visualized that mass education could be provided efficiently and easily. He accepted the idea that "the common people" could be taught "the most essential parts of education ... to read, write, and account ... at so early a period of life, that the greater part of those who are bred to the lowest occupations have time to acquire them before they can be employed in these occupations."[5] One reason that Smith envisioned so short a time frame for producing the educated man was that he had faith in the power of even the most rudimentary education to upgrade the individual: "There is scarce any man ... who by discipline, education and example may not be so impressed with regard to general rules, as to act upon almost every occasion with tolerable decency, and through the whole of his life to avoid any considerable degree of blame."[6]

Jeremy Bentham was a man obsessed with order and spent much of his time specifying the rules and regulations for his many imaginative schemes. Among his projects was one to teach young children to read, write, and think through the use of the British legal code.[7] He supposed the students would learn a bit of the law along with their letters. Bentham suggested a system of national education organized as a profit making company similar, he said, to the East India Company. He particularized the advantages to the public from the spread of instruction under his proposed plan: there would be improvements in the "faculty of self-maintenance, faculty of self-amusement, intellectual strength, moral health, military strength, faculty of pleasing, (and) religious affections." All of these benefits would be the outcome of the provision of "suitable instruction - instruction in all suitable points of art and knowledge."[8] Bentham claimed that as the individual grew internally, the society as a whole would benefit. Thus, Bentham, as Smith, adhered to the traditional positive externalities argument.

The Reverend T. R. Malthus maintained that much of the macroeconomic benefits of education centered around prudent procreation habits which an enlightened population would adopt. Thus, he expected education to raise the "standard of wretchedness" of the majority of the population. Furthermore, Malthus contended that education would do so *if* it included "the particular doctrines which it has fallen to (Malthus) more than any other man to bring home to the public mind."[9]

Malthus also advocated the role of education in promoting social stability. He noted that education "appears to have a considerable effect in the prevention of crimes, and the promotion of industry, morality, and regular conduct."[10] Besides increases in productivity and righteousness, education would reduce the chance of misguided rebellion, Malthus claimed. Educated men were less disposed to "insubordination and turbulence" and were aware of the evils which "ambitious demagogues" could cause.[11] Consequently, Malthus, as Smith before him, was cognizant of the place that education played in a democratic order: he thought that it enhanced "all the favorable consequences to be expected from civil and political liberty."[12]

Malthus, too, recognized the macroeconomic spillover effects of education. He recorded that "the raising of one person may actually contribute to the raising of others." Malthus continued, "also, his conduct ... tends to improve the condition of his fellow labourers."[13] He believed strongly in man's ability to teach others through imitation. Malthus, trained as a clergyman, could easily identify with the external effects that accrue to setting a good example.

David Ricardo and T. R. Malthus were friends and correspondents who shared many intellectual discussions. Although education and educational provision held no significant place in Ricardo's economic analysis, he could not remain oblivious to the population pressures emphasized by Malthus. When Ricardo cited "all the evils of a crowded population" he pointed out "the evil (which) proceeds from government, from the insecurity of property and from a want of education in all ranks of people."[14] An excess of population both caused and resulted from ignorant citizens, he discovered.

Ricardo attributed other macroeconomic benefits to education. First, he mentioned that education was powerful in directing similar action on the part of dissimilar men. In a letter to J. R. McCulloch he remarked: "The conduct of two different sets of men educated nearly in the same manner ... cannot be materially different."[15] Second, Ricardo endorsed the concept of increasing capital formation through education. From this he reasoned that education could serve as a catalyst to macroeconomic growth and social well-being. He predicted: "to be made happier (individuals) require only to be better governed and instructed, as the augmentation of capital, beyond the augmentation of people would be the inevitable result."[16] Into his macroeconomic analysis of the returns to education Ricardo incorporated the idea that because of education a nation would be able to increase its capital stock in a greater proportion than its increase in population. The end result of education, then, would be to forestall the certainty of the stationary state.

Jean Baptiste Say took a broader view of education than did Ricardo or Malthus when he remarked that government sponsorship of academies, libraries, public schools and museums was a necessary part of an expanding society. He decided that government could contribute to the creation of national wealth by "furthering the discovery of truth."[17] Since the work of the pure theorist was of greater benefit to the public than to the individual, Say held that it was not "extravagant for government to support academies and learned institutions in their capacity to extend as well as to store knowledge. In formulating this idea, Say expressed an early argument for government provision of goods with positive externalities in production.

In Say's expanded view "every advance of science is followed by an increase in social happiness," since eventually scientific discoveries were put to practical use.[18] He anticipated government aid in this endeavor by "helping to extend the application of human science to the supply of human wants."[19] Nevertheless, Say cautioned that, although government service was essential to gain these positive spillover benefits, care must be taken to avoid complacency, faction-making and prejudices which usually accompanied activities under government control.

James Mill proposed a macroeconomic argument for primary education based on the concept of universal justice. Philosophically he penned these words: "Till recently it was denied that intelligence was a desirable quality in the great body of people, and as intelligence is power, such is an unavoidable opinion in the breasts of those who think that the human race ought to consist of two classes, one that of the oppressors, another that of the oppressed." Mill continued his thought: "As we strive for an equal degree of justice, an equal degree of veracity, in the poor as in the rich, so ought we to strive for an equal degree of intelligence."[20] Mill compared the universal dissemination of knowledge to that of truth or justice - he believed that everyone should be accorded these in like measure.

Mill identified a flagrant source of injustice, the plight of pauper children. Their individual distress was a sign of a larger social malaise, Mill forewarned. He noted: "The children of the poor are observed to be in general brought up without education, abandoned to themselves, learning all the idle and disorderly habits which render men bad members of society."[21] This was additionally upsetting to Mill because he considered the macroeconomic effects of a good education on "the body of the people" so obvious that they must "appear perfectly trite" to all but the dullest thinkers. Mill's reflections on the social cost of denying education to poor children was articulated succinctly by another classical economist, Nassau Senior, when he wrote: "No country is so poor as to be unable to bear the expense of good elementary schools. Strictly speaking, it is not an expense. The money so employed is much more than repaid by the superiority in diligence, in skill, in economy, and in health."[22]

J. R. McCulloch, as James Mill, was vividly impressed by the condition of the untaught: "An ignorant and uneducated people, though possessed of all the materials and power necessary for the production of wealth, are uniformly sunk in poverty and barbarism: and until their mental powers begin to expand, and they learn to exercise the empire of mind over matter, the avenues of improvement are shut against them, and they have neither the power nor the wish to emerge from their degraded condition."[23] McCulloch maintained that the hopelessness that the uncultured experienced surfaced in anti-social activity: "nine-tenths of the misery and crime which afflict and disgrace society have their source in ignorance."[24]

Besides causing decreased productivity and increased crime, McCulloch discovered that the lack of education set workers against their employers and encouraged the workers to fault others for their lot in life. He had confidence that education would show the workers "how closely their interests are identified with those of their employers."[25] McCulloch's conclusion regarding education and the worker-employer relation was directly opposite that soon to be voiced by Marx and Engles. Also McCulloch expressed another opinion contrary to Marxian thought when he contended that education might make the poor realize that they themselves were the masters of their fate. He elaborated: an educated citizen would observe that "the most tolerant and liberal Government, and the best institutions, cannot shield them from poverty and degradation, without the exercise of a reasonable degree of forethought, frugality, and good conduct, on their part."[26] If there were general education, McCulloch would calculate its macroeconomic benefits "over the fortunes of the empire" as inestimable.

John Stuart Mill considered universal education ás a prerequisite to the establishment of a "tolerant and liberal Government" in a democracy. Mill was most vocal in asserting that education would help the mass of the people to "cultivate common sense," to form "sound practical judgment," and to bring about "balance" in the workers' political thought.[27] To the point, he specified that no person "should participate in the suffrage, without being able to read, write, and ... perform the common operation of arithmetic."[28] Mill was in awe of the uneducated majority; he realized that a democratic society needed "protection against the tyranny of the prevailing opinion and feeling; against the tendency of society to impose ... its own ideas and practices as rules of conduct on those who dissent from them."[29] Mill did not want the prevailing opinion to be an uncultivated one.

Moreover, Mill fervently desired mass participatory activity

40

in government. Deciding with others on some political action was a basic part of the individual's civic and moral education, Mill wrote, sounding a little like his father, James. The development of right thinking in the governmental sphere, was essential to a workable democratic system. Mill remarked that the individual learned to discharge political power in a democracy only by practicing it and he needed an education to be able to exercise his political rights. [30]

Civic responsibility was second to educational attainment in Mill's mind: "If society has neglected to discharge two solemn obligations, the more important and the more fundamental of the two must be fulfilled first: universal teaching must precede universal enfranchisement." [31] Education was required for "practical political activity" and citizen participation in this activity was a key element in a successful democratic macro-society. [32]

Mill, who ran afoul of the law early in his career by distributing birth control information, was firmly convinced of the power of education to yield macroeconomic benefits through the reduction of population pressures. He looked forward to universal education that would "keep the increase of population within proper limits." [33] As Malthus, Mill expected that education on population control would be a part of the general system of education: "For the purpose therefore of altering the habit of the labouring people, there is a need for twofold action. ... An effective national education of the children of the labouring class is the first thing needful; and coincidently with this, a system of measures which shall ... extinguish extreme poverty for one whole generation." [34] Mill's "system of measures" was actually the dissemination of practical information on family planning. Therefore, according to Mill, general education of pauper children and special education for their parents regarding methods of reducing the growth of population was a necessary combination for the eventual reduction of poverty. The need to break out of the circle of poverty caused by increases in population which outstripped increases in productivity was as obvious to Mill as to Ricardo. Ricardo forecast educational advance to raise productivity; additionally, Mill and Malthus foresaw the spread of education as a tool for reducing the rise in population growth. Mill also supplied the germ for the analysis of an income-consumption relation in the demand for education from the poor: "it is impossible effectively to teach an indigent population. And it is difficult to make those feel the value of comfort who have never enjoyed it." [35] Here he pointed out another element in the circle of poverty.

Mill championed "the general diffusion of intelligence among the people" for its "high economic value," [36] but he also

41

supported differences in educational levels among individuals. In a letter written in 1869, Mill gave his reader to ponder: "America surpasses all countries in the amount of mental cultivation which she has been able to make universal; but a high average level is not everything. There are wanted, I do not say a class, but a great number of persons of the highest degree of cultivation which the accumulated acquisitions of the human race make it possible to give them." [37] Mill fully expected macroeconomic spillovers from this arrangement as the influence of this cultivated group "rained down" on society to enhance the well-being of all. In an earlier work (1832), Mill criticized the "diffusion" of knowledge among so many students in colleges and universities. He wondered "whether our 'march of intellect' be not a march towards doing without intellect, and supplying our deficiency of giants by the united efforts of a constantly increasing multitude of dwarfs." [38]

Mill was unwilling to call for a "class" of superior intellectuals since he was acutely aware of the growing class consciousness among the middle and lower income groups. Universal basic education would not lower the educational attainment of the most intelligent group, Mill supposed, but would go a long way toward raising the literacy level of the most uneducated and impoverished people. Mill regarded basic education as a key that could unlock the riches of a full life to those who had been denied it for so long. He recommended that the working classes be taught all "which relates to human life and the ways of mankind; geography, voyages, and travels, manners and customs, and romances, which must tend to awaken their imagination and give them some of the meaning of self-devotion and heroism, in short, to unbrutalize them." [39] Here Mill suggested that the lower classes be given the cultural and esthetic values of the classes above them through education. This was the very type of education that Marx and Engels would claim the bourgeoisie were too "silly" to recognize as relevant to the future of a capitalistic society.

Mill did recognize the need for new ideas in education. If macroeconomic returns to primary education were to be maximized, all people ought to be participants in the educational plan. Mill's expectations for the education of the working class were surpassed only by his desire to open educational opportunities to women. The first schools for "young ladies" were not intended to transmit knowledge at all, but were instituted to serve as a vehicle for spreading refinement and morality. The earliest serious attempts at education for women in England occurred in the mid 1800s when the need to certify governesses arose. [40] Mill had been monitoring the progress of women in education since the beginning of his career. He expressed these thoughts to his confidante, Harriet Taylor: "It is not law, but education and custom" which make the difference in the roles of men and women in society. [41] In the break from traditional patterns, Mill judged that "the first and indispensable step ... is that she be so educated, as not to be dependent either on her father or her husband for subsistence." [42] Simple economics could be used to describe why the customary employment of the female in the home was a waste of resources, Mill said. He considered that large numbers of children could be cared for in nursery schools more efficiently by "persons trained in the profession of teaching" thereby reaping the economic gains of mass production. Teaching many children under the same roof need not reduce the amount of love that a babe received, Mill reasoned, since true maternal education was "the training of the affections," a natural part of the mothering process, not a special task that required constant attention and all of a mother's productive time. [43] Mill did not doubt that the habits ingrained in society were difficult to overcome, but he observed that there was hope since "the wisest and perhaps the quickest means to do away with the evils (of married life) is to be found in promoting education - as it is the means of all good ... ."[44]

Mill repeated many of these ideas on the education of women in his 1861 work, *The Subjection of Women*. Once again he re-called that opportunities for learning had been denied to women and resulted in the lack of "general knowledge - exactly the thing which education can best supply." [45] On the macroeconomic level, Mill visualized a "great accession to the intellectual power of the species" when women were "better and more completely edu-cated."[46] Although society would be much improved when women received education, Mill felt that a personal triumph for women would be clearly indicated: "the mere breaking down of the barrier would itself have an educational value of the highest note."[47]

To expedite the breakdown of the barriers in women's educa-tion, Mill bequeathed the large sum of six thousand pounds, nearly half of his entire estate, to this cause. Being a free market economist, he recognized the value of monetary incentives, and so, three thousand pounds of the bequest was earmarked for the first British university to allow women to earn degrees. The remaining three thousand pounds was reserved to endow scholar-ships exclusively for female students. [48]

Herbert Spencer, too, contemplated the macroeconomic effects of universal education. However, his observations differed from those of most of the classical economic thinkers of his time. He blatantly opposed the classical contention that basic education would produce more law abiding citizens and, thus, lead to a reduction in crime. Spencer asserted that although most criminals were found to have little education, they were also found to have other characteristics in common, such as badly ventilated rooms and dirty shirts. Spencer argued logically that "ignorance ... simply indicates the presence of crime-producing influences, and can no more be called the cause of crime than the falling of a barometer can be called the cause of rain."[49] He recalled that men of religion had been trying unsuccessfully to cure crime for centuries and that it would be truly amazing if educators could do it in fifty years; in his own colorful words: "If hopes of eternal happiness and terrors of eternal damnation fail to make human beings virtuous, it is hardly likely that the commendations and reproofs of the schoolmaster will succeed."[50]

Spencer's assertion regarding the relation between education and crime has been upheld by several modern authors. John O. Nelson studied the contemporary statistical correlation between crime and education and he concluded that there is ample evidence against the idea that education reduces crime in modern society.[51] Murray Rothbard astutely observed that "an educated person can commit all the crimes that are committed by the uneducated; but education provides the means to commit many crimes that are simply beyond the reach of the illiterate and uneducated (e.g. forgery, embezzlement, electronic bugging)."[52] And, lastly, E. G. West inspected the crime-education relation in its nineteenth century milieu; he concluded that the statistical evidence collected to support the crime reducing argument for education was very weak. West reported that lacking the ability to control for extraneous variables, it was possible that statistics gathered in the 1800s might well demonstrate that "ignorance and crime" may not have been "cause and effect but concomitant results of the same cause."[53]

In Spencer's view the character of the individual was not easily changed by education or by anything else. He presented the unique idea that macroeconomic harm might occur "by artificially increasing intelligence without regard to character."[54] Spencer made specific reference to the common man's reaction to tabloid sensationalism: "The slumbering instincts of the barbarian have been awakened by a demoralized Press, which would have done comparatively little had not the artificial spread of intellectual culture brought the masses under its influence."[55] Moreover, Spencer characterized the misplaced education of the masses as a breeding ground for anarchial ideas. He reflected on the type of person who instigated political revolution: "Besides the constitutionally criminal, those who are led into these erroneous beliefs, and violent acts in pursuance of them, are the educated. Without those facilities for communication which reading and writing and a certain amount of knowledge give them, there could not be formed these schools of anarchy."[56] Spencer, contrary to Mill, thought basic education furnished by the state to all, regardless of their "character", would cause more harm than good in the macroeconomy.[57]

In coming to this conclusion Spencer relied on his omni-present theory of social evolution. This theory supported his educational ideas as he maintained that mass state education "interferes with natural selection." He persisted, "if those of the lower ranks are left to get culture for their children as best they may ... it must follow that the children of the superior will be advantaged."[58] Spencer, writing more than a century after Adam Smith, depended upon classic natural law philosophy to con-demn state education. In his view the matter was simple: state education was a transgression against "natural law"; therefore, it should be abolished.[59]

Marx and Engles anticipated the macroeconomic changes from universal education which would alter social relationships. Engles stressed that "society gains more from educated than from ignorant, uncultured members" but more importantly, he empha-sized that "an educated proletariat will not be disposed to remain in the present (oppressed) condition."[60] Once again Engles picked up the theme of gradual change rather than violent, disruptive change. He averred that, led by educational reforms, the ground work for "the calm composure necessary for the peaceful transformation of society" would be in place.[61]

The educational scheme that Marx and Engles envisioned would be all encompassing. Since their plan called for infant education, the learning environment of the masses would be directed from the earliest years and, as a side benefit, parents would be freed from the responsibility of having to provide continuous care for their children. Their reformed system con-tained "education (for) all children, as soon as they are old enough to do without the first maternal care, in national insti-tutions at the expense of the nation."[62] In promoting this plan, Engles felt he was striking a blow for parental independence. Because the state would have direct control of the child's edu-cation, it would have one less reason to become involved with parents. This would allow, according to Engles, the "relation between the sexes (to be) a private affair in which society has no call to interfere."[63]

Another classical macroeconomic change which education could render would be an increase in the national product through a more intensive use of the resource, labor; Marx directed that the proposed educational provision "will, in the case of every child over a given age, combine productive labour with instruction and gymnastics."[64] Marx maintained that this educational technique would certainly be "one of the methods of adding to the efficiency of production," but more importantly, he was aware that it was "the *only* method of producing *fully developed human beings*."[65]

45

Marx and Engles freely admitted education's power to affect the whole man and through this the whole of mankind. In this they were not far from a Smith-Bentham-Mill interpretation of the efficacy of education to alter the life of even the most impoverished individual. Moreover, the Marx-Engles closely monitored educational environment could have been part of a James Mill plan for education. Finally, the infant school idea was certainly a favorite of J. S. Mill, as well as of Marx and Engles.

Henry Fawcett, writing toward the end of the era, summarized, in part, the macroeconomic ideas of his economic predecessors.[66] He affirmed that widespread schooling would raise industrial productivity while increasing labor mobility. This would improve both the quality and quantity of the national product, he reasoned. Fawcett thought that education would lessen intemperance and provide a greater level of individual well-being, partially due to the spread of knowledge about sanitary conditions. However the greatest good which Fawcett anticipated from the extension of education throughout the community was the unfolding of higher forms of social development. He foresaw the lessening of the antagonism between employer and employee as a direct consequence of educating the laborer. Fawcett even predicted the general Marxian scenario for the future of the educated masses: he envisioned a major macroeconomic change, the formation of a new type of economic system. Educated workers could rise to the level of partners in the industrial process; the workers could become capitalists.

As Fawcett, Henry Sidgwick considered that the future of society would contain changes in the traditional worker-industrialist relation. Sidgwick determined that education would be a pivotal part of this change. He knew that education was one method of achieving the redistribution of income. Furthermore, the macroeconomic benefits of education which "tend to strengthen on the whole, rather than weaken, habits of energetic industry, thrift, and self-help in the individual assisted" worked from within the individual, upgrading his skills and his self-confidence.[67] Only when men were assured of the opportunity to expand their productive capabilities would they be ready participants in a free market system, Sidgwick explained. Education and income redistribution would hasten this objective.

NOTES

1. Adam Smith, *An Inquiry into the Nature and Causes of the Wealth of Nations*, ed. Edwin Cannan (New York, 1937), p. 739.

2. Ibid.

3. Ibid.

4. Ibid.

5. Ibid., p. 305.

6. Adam Smith, *The Theory of Moral Sentiments*, ed. D. D. Raphall and A. L. Macfie (Oxford, 1976), p. 230.

7. See: Mary Mack, *Jeremy Bentham: An Odyssey of Ideas* (London, 1963), p. 313.

8. Jeremy Bentham, "Outline of a work entitled Pauper Management Improved," *The Works of Jeremy Bentham*, ed. John Bowring (New York, 1962), p. 395.

9. Quoted in Warren J. Samuels, "The Classical Theory of Economic Policy," *Southern Economic Journal*, Vol. 31 (2), pp. 96-97.

10. T. R. Malthus, *An Essay on the Principle of Population*, 3rd ed. (London, 1806), p. 259.

11. T. R. Malthus, *Principles of Political Economy*, 2nd ed. (New York, 1964), p., 227.

12. Ibid.

13. Malthus, *Principles*, p. 474; quoted in Pierre N. V. Tu, "The Classical Political Economists and Education," *Kyklos*, Vol. 22, 1969, p. 695.

14. David Ricardo, *The Works and Correspondence of David Ricardo*, ed. Piero Sraffa (Cambridge, 1952), Vol. VII, pp. 359-60.

15. Quoted in Samuels, p. 96.

16. David Ricardo, *The Principles of Political Economy and Taxation*, Everyman's Library Edition (New York, 1969), p. 56.

17. J. B. Say, *A Treatise on Political Economy* (New York, 1964), p. 201.

18. Ibid., p. 432.

19. Ibid., p. 201.

20. Quoted in W. H. G. Armytage, *Four Hundred Years of English Education* (Cambridge, 1970), p. 101.

21. James Mill, *On Education*, ed. W. H. Burston (Cambridge, 1969), p. 41.

22. Marion Bowley, *Nassau W. Senior and Classical Economics* (Chicago, 1937), p. 264.

23. John R. McCulloch, *The Principles of Political Economy*, 5th ed. (New York, 1965), p. 67.

24. Quoted in E. G. West, "Private versus Public Education, A Classical Economic Dispute," in *The Classical Economists and Economic Policy*, ed. A. W. Coats (London, 1971), p. 134.

25. Quoted in Samuels, p. 97.

26. Ibid.

27. John Stuart Mill, *Principles of Political Economy*, ed. William Ashley (Fairfield, 1976), p. 380.

28. John Stuart Mill, *Considerations on Representative Government* (Southbend, Indiana, 1962), p. 116.

29. Maurice Cranston, *John Stuart Mill* (London, 1958), p. 18.

30. See: Dennis F. Thompson, *John Stuart Mill and Representative Government* (Princeton, N. J., 1976), p. 44.

31. Quoted in John M. Robson, *The Improvement of Mankind* (London, 1968), p. 210.

32. Quoted in R. J. Halliday, *John Stuart Mill* (New York, 1976), p. 98.

33. Mill, *Considerations*, p. 381.

34. Quoted in Michael St. John Packe, *The Life of John Stuart Mill* (New York, 1954), p. 301.

35. Mill, *Principles*, p. 381.

36. Ibid.

37. Packe, p. 482.

38. Ibid., p. 133.

39. Edward Alexander, *Matthew Arnold and John Stuart Mill* (New York, 1965), p. 289.

40. See: "Schoolmistresses and Headmistresses: Elites and Education in Nineteenth Century England" by Joyce Senders Pederson in *The Journal of British Studies*, Vol. 15 (1), pp. 133-162.

41. F. A. Hayek, *John Stuart Mill and Harriet Taylor: Their Correspondence and Subsequent Marriage* (Chicago, 1951), p. 63.

42. Ibid., p. 65.

43. Ibid., p. 67.

44. Ibid., p. 67.

45. John Stuart Mill and Harriet Taylor, *Essays in Sex Equality*, ed. Alice S. Rossi (Chicago, 1970), p. 191.

46. Ibid., p. 221.

47. Ibid., p. 222.

48. Packe, p. 500.

49. Herbert Spencer, *Social Statics* (New York, 1954), p. 310.

50. Ibid., p. 313.

51. E. G. West, *Nonpublic School Aid* (Lexington, Massachusetts, 1965), p. 106.

52. Murray Rothbard, "Total Reform: Nothing Less" in E. G. West, *Nonpublic School Aid*, p. 106.

53. Ibid., p. 133.

54. Herbert Spencer, *Facts and Comments* (New York, 1902), p. 84.

55. Ibid., p. 89.

56. Ibid., p. 90.

57. There are some people today who hold that universal education yields negative externalities, for example, the members of the Amish religion. See: West, *Nonpublic School Aid*, p. 105.

58. Spencer, *Facts and Comments*, p. 67.

59. David Wilshire, *The Social and Political Thought of Herbert Spencer* (Oxford, 1978), p. 49.

60. Karl Marx and Friedrich Engles, *Collected Works* (New York, 1975), Vol. IV, p. 527.

61. Ibid.

62. Marx and Engles, *Collected Works* Vol. VI, p. 351.

63. Ibid.

64. Karl Marx, *Capital* (Moscow, 1948), Vol. I, p. 453.

65. Ibid.

66. Henry Fawcett, *Pauperism: Its Causes and Remedies* (New York, 1971), p. 125.

67. Henry Sidgwick, *Principles of Political Economy* (London, 1883), p. 537.

CHAPTER IV

THE CLASSICAL CONCEPTS OF THE MICROECONOMICS OF EDUCATION, INCLUDING OPPORTUNITY AND DEMAND

INTRODUCTION

Since the attainment of a high level of national output was a classical macroeconomic goal, the economic writers looked to education to help meet that objective. But education obviously did more than foster a healthy economy; it also improved the prosperity of the individual worker. To investigate this phenomenon, the classical political economists emphasized the microeconomic analysis of education. In this study, the individual's use of education to increase his own productivity and, as a consequence, his own income, claimed the center of attention.

Just as there were macroeconomic spillover benefits to education, there were also microeconomic spillover benefits. Truly, the educated man received an increase in wages relative to his uneducated counterpart, but the political economists also noted that education caused an upgrading of personal happiness and contentment. It was not surprising that the educated citizen enjoyed the intellectual pleasures of the world outside of the dreary work place when he was introduced to their existence. Once the worker knew that there was more to life than just punching the clock, his entire existence took on new meaning. Moreover, the reduction in ill-health due to instruction in rudimentary techniques of sanitation made living more pleasurable for the individual and for his family.

One major obstacle to the dissemination of education among the laboring classes was the true or opportunity cost of going to school. The meager fees charged for school attendance were rarely cited as the stumbling block to the poor child's education. Rather the chief deterrent was the income that the child's family lost when he was in school and not in the factory working. For many families who relied on the wages of all family members for sustenance, the opportunity cost of education was prohibitively high. At the heart of this issue was the notion of the fundamental right of the child to education. When offering a solution to this problem, the economists were divided in their opinions.

Having considered the microeconomic benefits of education and the difficulties which arose because of opportunity cost, the political economists were prepared to present their ideas on the economic demand they perceived for education in their time. One thing was very clear – as the century progressed, the demand for education had been changing. Technical and social events

51

had begun to encourage rather than discourage school attendance. As the early economic writers predicted, when the microeconomic returns from education were made plain to the worker, he responded in a logical fashion by demanding more schooling. The political economist took up the investigation of the phenomenon of changing educational demand.

THE MICROECONOMIC RETURNS TO EDUCATION

Adam Smith's approach to the microeconomic returns to education was basic. His first principle of education was: education is preparation for "the real business of the world, the business which is to employ (the pupils) during the remainder of their days."[1] The emphasis on the employment aspect of education led Smith to explore the reasons behind wage differentials between workers. He presumed that the original endowment of each human being was very similar since every man must care for his own survival needs and, surely, Smith thought, nature would provide each person with the tools to do so. Smith remarked: "all must have ... the same duties to perform, and the same work to do, ... there could have been no such difference of employment as could alone give occasion to any great difference in talents."[2] Therefore, Smith reasoned that most of the differences between men were due to external influences; he penned that "the difference between the most dissimilar characters, between the philosopher and a common street porter, for example, seems to arise not so much from nature as from habit, custom, and education."[3]

A worker who had been educated to a certain trade should be rewarded commensurate with the extra effort expended upon his education, Smith decided. Specifically, he recounted that "there are many acts which require more extensive knowledge than is to be got during the time of apprenticeship. A blacksmith and weaver may learn their business well enough without any previous knowledge of mathematics, but a watch-maker must be acquainted with several sciences in order to undertake his business well, such as arithmetic, geometry, and astronomy, with high regard to the equation of time, and their wages must be high in order to compensate the additional expense."[4] In general terms, Smith concluded simply that "the wages of labour vary with the easiness and cheapness or the difficulty and expense of learning the business ... . The difference between the wages of skilled labour and those of common labour is founded upon this principle."[5]

Smith promoted the idea of the ability of education to enhance human capital formation. He considered that human capital, just like physical capital would be rewarded in the marketplace: "A man educated at the expense of much labour and time to any of those employments which require extraordinary dexterity and skill, may be compared to one of those expensive machines."[6] Smith went on, "The work which he learns to per-form, it must be expected, over and above the usual wages of common labour, will replace to him the whole expense of his education, with at least the ordinary profits of an equally valuable capital."[7] Investment in human capital and physical capital were so similar that Smith reasoned that the returns to both types would be equalized in the market.

Smith related the higher expected returns to skilled labor to product market equilibrium. He believed that the promise of higher rewards would serve as a stimulus to the workers' self-improvement in the skills in high demand. Smith thought that when higher wages were paid for jobs which required specific training there would be "sufficient encouragement to the labourer, and the commodity will be cultivated in proportion to the demand."[8] Smith imagined that the natural harmony of the equilibrating free market price for skilled labor would call forth enough workers who would be willing to invest in training to meet the rising product demand.

However, Smith recalled a curious exception to his education-determined free market equilibrium rule when he men-tioned some types of work which require a large outlay on edu-cation but where the rewards were on average not enough to offset the expenditure. Smith noted "in general, this is the case in all the liberal arts, because after they have spent a long time in their education, it is ten to one if ever they make anything by it."[9] But because the chances of an individual succeeding were small, the absolute wages in these professions had to be large enough to overcome the uncertainties involved: "Their wages, therefore, must be higher in proportion to the expense they have been at, the risk of not living long enough, and the risk of not having dexterity enough to manage their business."[10] Smith as-tutely observed at this point that practitioners of the liberal arts usually had a hard time coping with the realities of the business world, especially with the generation of a demand adequate enough to earn a living and with the techniques necessary to keep their businesses in the black. Chief among these indi-viduals was the lawyer (of course) and Smith gave this review of his plight: "Among the lawyers there is not one among twenty that attains such knowledge and dexterity in his business as enables him to get back the expenses of his education, and many of them never make the price of their gown, as we say."[11] So, Smith queried, what would possibly encourage an intelligent person to enter an occupation where the cost of entry is high and the probability of adequate returns is limited? His own response was: "it is the eminence of the profession, and not the money made of it, that is the temptation for applying to it, and the dignity of that rank is to be considered as a part of what is made by it."[12]

In addition to education, Smith included the idea of risk in his analysis of wage determination. If the risks involved with an occupation were high, wages would be high to compensate for these risks. Smith wondered what enticed individuals to take the risk of not earning enough to live comfortably, especially in the legal profession. His solution was that nonmonetary rewards, too, encourage labor supply to an occupation; the dignity or eminence of a profession will stimulate supply even if the demand is only enough to provide barely satisfactory living arrangements for many practitioners.

Ricardo appeared ambiguous in his feelings about the microeconomic effects of education on the worker. On the one hand he wrote that, "Whatever inequality there might originally have been in them (kinds of labour), whatever the ingenuity, skill or time necessary for the acquirement of one species of manual dexterity more than another, it ... can have little effect ... on the relative value of commodities.[13] Here, of course, Ricardo indicated that labor quality was not important in wage determination and, therefore, in the determination of product prices. However, later on, Ricardo penned: "It is not difficult to conceive that with better education and improved habits, a day's labour may become much more valuable ... ."[14] Ricardo made this second comment in a discussion on wage determination and the natural price of labor. With such contradictory statements about the microeconomic effects of education, perhaps it would be best to notice that Ricardo spent very little time exploring the place of education in the economy and did not systematically record his thoughts on its implications on the individual.

Jeremy Bentham was as thorough in his educational thought as in his other designs. Bentham proposed Chrestomathia, "a day school for the extension of the new system of instruction to the higher branches of learning for the use of the middling and higher ranks in life."[15] Since this was to be a school funded by subscription, he advertised the purpose of the school as an augmentation in "the quantity of useful knowledge possessed by the middle class."[16] But because the school relied on paying customers for its maintenance, Bentham cited the specific microeconomic improvements which could be expected from attendance at this institution: "The only manifestly natural and probable results are, improvement in respect of health, domestic economy, and personal comfort; a more extensive disposition than at present to look for amusement and recreation in art, science, or literature, in preference to sensuality and indolence."[17]

Bentham stressed the consumption benefits which would accrue to his middle class students in Chrestomathia. They would be happier because they were healthier, more intelligent, and able to appreciate the finer pleasures of life. Yet Bentham did not neglect children in lower socio-economic classes. For these students, Bentham had devised the National Charity Company's educational plan. These scholars, too, would receive specific microeconomic benefits from their education. There would be benefits in consumption as they would have the advantages of "comfort, continuance of existence (nourishment), health, strength, cleanliness and personal security."[18] But, in addition, the pauper children would be apprenticed at an early age to learn a skill which would be useful throughout their lifetimes. Bentham summed up his National Charity Company educational philosophy: "The business of education includes the business of providing occupations of one kind or another, for filling up in some way or other the time of the individual to be educated."[19] Bentham was determined that the scare resource, time, should be used to the utmost in his educational plan and that his students' education should provide them with richer, more fruitful lives.

J. B. Say sympathized with the "plodding mechanic" who spent all of his time in the work place. Adam Smith had written of the stultifying effects of the division of labor and Say's remarks expanded on that theme. He observed that without "a certain degree of education of reading, of reflection while at work, and of intercourse with persons of his own condition," the mechanic would remain narrow and crude.[20] More important, Say pointed out, were the long run effects of depriving the worker of education. He forecasted that a low level of achievement would be passed on to the next generation because the mechanic earned mere subsistence and could only afford to rear his family up to the same level.

When John Ramsey McCulloch concentrated on the human capital aspects of education, he summed up the elements that make up the laborer: "Man is as much the product of previous outlays of wealth expended upon his subsistence, education, etc. as any of the instruments constructed by his agency."[21] McCulloch often fused the microeconomic and macroeconomic aspects of education. He underscored the importance of human capital formation since an increase in individual productivity led to a rise in the national output. McCulloch set down: "Much stress is ... justly laid on the efficiency of the machines which man has constructed to assist his undertakings; but he is himself the most important of all machines, and every addition made to his skill and dexterity is an acquisition of the utmost importance."[22] He realized the macroeconomic effects of microeconomic advance.

John Stuart Mill, in a statement sounding very much like

Smith and Bentham, wrote: "The main branch of the education of human beings is their habitual employment."[23] Additionally, Mill considered how differing levels of educational attainment affected the wages which different employments received. He pondered the problem of "a clerk from whom nothing is required but the mechanical labour of copying, (who) gains more than an equivalent for his mere exertion if he receives the wages of a bricklayer's labourer."[24] Mill attributed this discrepancy not to the arduousness of cerebral labor but to "monopoly, the small degree of education required being not yet even so generally diffused as to call forth the natural number of competitors ... ."[25] In another passage, Mill reported on the microeconomic effects on wages of excluding much of the population from education: "The number of persons fitted to direct and superintend any industrial enterprise, or even to execute any process which cannot be reduced almost to an affair of memory and routine, is always far short of the demand; as is evident from the enormous difference between salaries paid to such persons, and the wages of ordinary labour."[26] Mill cautioned the politicians of England to take note of this situation in forming their educational policy.

Yet Mill was optimistic about the ability of education to break the monopolistic barriers into higher paying jobs. He thought that social change would bring about changes in the demand for education as more of the laboring population began to recognize its microeconomic value. Mill penned: "Since reading and writing have been brought within the reach of a multitude, the monopoly price of the lower grade of educated employments has greatly fallen, the competition for them having been increased in an almost incredible degree."[27] However, Mill went on to warn the worker that unless the increase in education were coupled with a decrease in population pressures, the newly received income benefits would surely be negated.

Nassau Senior waxed eloquent when describing the microeconomic consequences of education to the children of the poor describing education as "the most effectual means of raising (the poor) from the condition of pauperism to that of industrial independence."[28] Education was the key to freedom for innumerable impoverished people, Senior claimed.

Senior also used the human capital approach to education as J. R. McCulloch had done. In this he employed his famous abstinence theory of capital accumulation explaining that funds expended for the accumulation of capital will be returned to the investor with a reward for delayed consumption. As applied to human capital he felt that "the greater part of the remuneration for skilled labor is the reward for the abstinence implied by a considerable expenditure on the labourer's education."[29] His abstinence theory held for human, as well as physical, capital,

Senior presumed.

Finally, Senior approached the consumption returns from education in a rather unique way. Unlike other writers who stressed increased health or personal satisfaction from intellectual growth, Senior viewed education as a consumption good for parents. Senior imagined that "to witness a son's daily improvement is, ... one of the greatest sources of immediate gratification. The expense incurred for that purpose is as much repaid by immediate enjoyment as that which is incurred to obtain the most transitory pleasures."[30] Senior saw the short-run consumption benefits and the long-run productive returns to education.

Marx and Engles would subsequently take issue with Senior's idea that parental joy could be an inducement to good education in a bourgeoisie dominated capitalistic society. Under the capitalistic system, they held, "children (were) transformed into simple articles of commerce and instruments of labour."[31] In fact, Marx and Engles argued that the parents themselves were to blame for allowing conditions to deteriorate to such a state: the destruction of the family had already been completed "by the action of Modern Industry." Their strongest hope for change lay in the removal of the child from the home so that he might be educated; so that he might one day personally enjoy some of the advantages of education. Parental happiness did not necessarily bring justice to children, Marx deduced.

Marx and Engles were astonished at the poor reception of this portion of their educational plan. They were quick to retort that they were not the original authors of the concept of education outside the home. This aged "evil" had been scorned by no less than Adam Smith himself. Using much of recent past European educational history as evidence, they reacted to their accusers: "The Communists have not invented the intervention of society in education."[32] However, they desired "to alter the character of the intervention, and to rescue education from the influence of the ruling class."[33] Part of their conception of the new education was an education in which the individual, himself, and not his parents or his class, determined his place in the future of society.

Engles pictured the education of the individual lasting until he "is capable of emerging as an independent member of society."[34] When the individual had gathered "at the expense of the state" the education and skills necessary to make him both satisfied with his own accomplishments and a productive part of the economy, then the microeconomic goals of education would be fulfilled, Engles decided. Engles saw his demand for a thorough education for all individuals as more than an expression of social necessity; he viewed universal education as "as act of justice ...

for clearly, every man has the right to the full development of his abilities and society wrongs him twice over when it makes ignorance a necessary consequence of poverty."[35]

Henry Fawcett presented a parallel thought when he said that children who lacked education were unable to use their productive capabilities to the fullest. He observed children of all ages in the streets of the cities and thought that the hours spent idle on street corners was a personal, as well as a social, waste. Without education, these individuals had no productive use for their time nor did they know how to enjoy their leisure. Fawcett wrote that "thousands have so little to do that spare time is a burden to them."[36]

Fawcett employed the tools of early microeconomic analysis to explain the trade-off between the hours worked by children in the factories and the fields, and the hours they spent in school. He presumed that the supply curve of hours offered for work by children would shift outward as they took more work and less schooling. Since Fawcett assumed this curve to be relatively inelastic, he reasoned that the rise in the supply price for children's labor would offset the reduction in hours offered, so that the total income loss would be less than "at first might be suspected." Second, with children providing fewer hours to the labor force, more hours of work were available for adult workers. Moreover, since adults commanded higher wages than children, total family income might possibly increase, not decrease, when children replaced work time with school time. However, Fawcett realized that free mobility between labor markets required that school attendance rules be on a national or regional level, rather than on a local level. If some localities legislated school attendance, while other did not, the higher child wages and more readily available hours for adult work in one place could be filled by people of all ages of neighboring localities who were attracted by the wage differentials.[37] This would negate all of the expected income benefits which Fawcett had decided could accrue to the substitution of school for work.

OPPORTUNITY COST OF EDUCATION

School attendance was a substantial problem well into the nineteenth century. In 1861, the Newcastle Commission reported that sixty-six percent of school age children were working rather than attending school.[38] At this time, those children who did attend school did not stay long. The average length of time in school was only 2.55 years, so the level of education received was truly minimal. Part of the problem was the relative ease with which work could be obtained. Also, if there were strict child labor codes in one area, a neighboring area would gladly hire the unemployed children. Rural and urban employers realized a cheap resource in the form of child labor, and they were not eager to forego it.

The earnings that children could generate were often the difference between survival and destitution for their families. In the 1860s and 1870s, boys and girls could earn 7 to 12 shillings per week in the cotton mills while their parents could earn approximately 16 to 18 shillings. At the same time, children of both sexes could make 3 to 4 shillings per week in agriculture and adults could make 9 to 16 shillings in the same occupation. It is noteworthy that during the same decade, a "typical" workman in London could provide a comparably comfortable living for a family of moderate size on an income of 21 shillings per week.[39] Of course, this level of comfort declined as the size of the household rose.

Adam Smith clearly recognized the opportunity cost of sending a child to school in a country where child labor was productive. Smith noticed that "the common people ... have little time to spare for education. Their parents can scarce afford to maintain them even in infancy. As soon as they are able to work, they must apply to some trade by which they can earn their subsistence."[40] He knew a reason for this condition: "In rich and commercial nations the division of labour, having reduced all trades to very simple operations, affords an opportunity of employing children very young."[41] As a consequence, "in the commercial parts of England," Smith remarked, "a boy of six or seven years of age at Birmingham can gain his threepence or sixpence a day; thus their education is neglected." By contrast, Smith wrote, in Scotland where "the division of labour is not far advanced, even the meanest porter can read and write because the price of education is cheap, and a parent can employ his child no other way at six or seven years of age."[42] The "actions of Modern Industry" had created the circumstances in which the value of a child's labor was greater than the value of his mental growth.

Smith attributed the lack of schooling of young children primarily to the alternative work opportunities provided by the division of labor. But he perceived another redoubtable consequence from the division of labor: he believed that the natural balance in family relations was altered as children went to work rather than to school. Smith commented: "But, besides this want of education, there is another great loss which attends the putting boys too soon to work. The boy begins to find that his father is obliged to him, and therefore throws off his authority. When he is grown up he has no ideas with which he can amuse himself. When he is away from his work he must betake himself to drunkenness and riot."[43] Moreover, Smith felt that rebellious, insolent, uneducated young men were the cause of social unrest. They lacked the stabilizing ideas which were normally imparted to them through the educational process. Smith sadly concluded that in the "commercial parts of England, the tradesmen are for the most part in this despicable condition. ... So it may very justly be said that the people who clothe the whole world are in rags themselves." [44]

Nassau Senior was also concerned with the high opportunity cost of education for some parents. He divided the society into two groups of potential scholars and compared the opportunity cost of schooling between the two groups. The first group, those whose parents or friends could afford to pay the whole expense of their education, had a very low opportunity cost of schooling. Senior imagined that this cost could easily be zero or even negative, since the children of this group had no source of alternative employment; in fact, their parents were eager to send them to school. Senior made this observation: "To a tradesman, a clergyman, or a professional man, children are a mere encumbrance; they earn no wages, they require attendance. Their absence at school is a relief." [45] In addition, Senior noted that the tendency of parents in this class to over-educate their individual children had a negative social effect. The eagerness of a parent "to give his children at least the education of his own rank" had often over-stocked professions with practitioners and had as a consequence lowered the average remuneration to those professions quite significantly. [46] Senior was willing to admit that the state might be partially to blame for the tendency toward over-education among the members of this class. State requirements which necessitated a minimum of knowledge or skill "for permission to exercise some profession or for the Civil Service" caused students to remain within the school system for excessive lengths of time. [47] Senior decried the waste of resources which occurred with these inefficient state regulations.

A second group of children who were ready for education, Senior pointed out, were the children of the laboring class whose parents or friends could afford to pay a portion of their educational expenses. The fact that they could afford to do so, did not mean that they always chose to do so. Unlike the children of the upper and middle classes, the children of the laboring class did have alternative uses for their time. Their labor was necessary for household chores and the money earned outside the home was often a crucial part of the family's income. Senior remarked: "In a labourer's family the children are the servants;" and "a still greater sacrifice (for schooling) is that of the child's wages." [48] The contrast between the opportunity cost of education for this group and that of the upper classes was striking. For the higher income group, the opportunity cost was often negligible, whereas, for the lower income group, the opportunity cost of education was frequently prohibitively high.

John Stuart Mill concurred with Senior's feelings regarding working parents who depended upon the income generated by their children. Mill judged that while some parents might neglect their children's education out of indifference, and others might neglect it out of greed, the most desperate case was that of those parents who had "really urgent pecuniary needs" and could not help but deny their children adequate education because of them.

Senior went beyond Mill, however, and accused parents of violating the basic rights of their offspring when they denied their child schooling because of excessively high opportunity cost of education. He fostered the idea that just as a child had the right to food, he also had a right to education. Senior insisted that, "It cannot be too often repeated that the child is as much entitled to protection as any other member of society. His mind is as much entitled to protection as his body. One is no more to be starved or depraved than the other."[49] Parents who sent their children to work instead of school were anti-social Senior judged: although society may "refuse to compel the parent to educate his child," society is not exempt "from the duty of seeing that the child is educated."[50] Senior stopped short of explicitly demanding compulsory education laws, but he did point out the social and individual costs of allowing poor parents to decide whether or not their children should receive education. More basically, he realized that denying education to pauper children was a social injustice since there was nothing which sustained pauperism more than ignorance.

In direct contrast to Senior's ideas on the rights of children was the view of Herbert Spencer. Spencer stoutly denied the contention that the child's rights were violated if he were not given educational opportunities. It is interesting that the logic for his denial was based on liberty: "What we call rights are merely arbitrary subdivisions of the general liberty to exercise the faculties; and that only can be called an infringement of rights which actually diminishes this liberty -- cuts off a previously existing power to pursue the objects of desire."[51] A careless parent did not do this, Spencer said, because the child's liberty to exercise his faculties was still intact. He maintained that "omitting instruction in no way takes from a child's freedom to do whatsoever it wills in the best way it can."[52] Spencer expressed the outside limits of the noninterventionist's argument.

THE DEMAND FOR EDUCATION

In the eighteenth and nineteenth centuries there were influences other than the opportunity cost of schooling which affected the demand for education. Among these were ill health, migratory work, and inclement weather. But, by and large, the most important deterrent to the demand for education, other than income foregone, was parental indifference. Often this took the form of open hostility. Parents, frequently of a conservative nature, held a poor opinion of the educational system and what it could offer them and their children. It was not until the end of the 1800s, when school quality began to rise, that the general parental view of schooling began to soften.

Untaught as youths, eager adults had begun to exhibit the desire to learn to read and write for their own sake. [54] At first, there was a strong motivation to be able to read the scriptures in a religious environment. Then, between 1840 and 1870, cheap books of a "vulgar" character appeared as the result of technological printing improvements. These inexpensive "romances" were an instant hit and were a prime encouragement to those who could not read to become literate. Furthermore, at this time, postal rate reform had reduced the cost of mailing letters which promoted the use of writing. Consequently, the utilization of the mails rose markedly during this period. [55] The working class had started to see the importance of education as a consumption good.

James Mill was quite taken with the "rapid progress which the love of education is making among the lower orders in England." In 1813, he claimed to have observed firsthand and to have researched the educational conditions in the city and the countryside. Mill was pleased to report that "even around London, in a circle of fifty miles radius, which is far from the most instructed and virtuous part of the kingdom, there is hardly a village that has not something of a school." Not only did the facilities for education readily exist, Mill reported, but they were effective since the children of both sexes know "more or less" how to read and write. Mill went on to attest to the almost sacrificial devotion to education on the part of English parents as he described the "families in which, for weeks together, not an article of sustenance but potatoes had been used, yet for every child the hard-earned sum was provided to send them to school." [56]

The observations of Nassau Senior and the Newcastle Commission of the late 1850s were not nearly as rosy as Mill's perceptions. One conclusion that Senior drew from his thorough examination of the educational system was that education could not be defined in a uniform manner, that different people thought of education differently. He reported: "Education is indefinite; it may begin at any age after three. It may end at any age before 21. It may be merely nominal as it appears to be in many of the private schools, of the endowed schools, and of the factory schools; or it may be as good as it is in the best of public schools."[57] In order to address the problem of educational demand, some common idea of what education is must be established, Senior reasoned.

Another fact that Senior gleaned from his study was that the demand for education was definitely distinct from that for other goods. He recognized that "its pecuniary results are distant and uncertain." Also, the user of education, the student, was normally not a voluntary consumer: "The child does not ask for it; in most cases it had rather be without it."[58] A third observation from Senior's research was that to the very poor, education was a good with a high income elasticity of demand. He opined, quite unlike James Mill: "The supply of education will not be allowed to interfere with the supply of food, clothing, fuel, or lodging. It is the expense that will be most frequently stinted, most frequently intermitted and the most frequently withdrawn."[59]

John Stuart Mill was also concerned about the lack of demand for education on the part of some members of society. Mill remonstrated: "If society lets any considerable number of its members grow up mere children, incapable of being acted on by rational consideration of distant motives, society has itself to blame for the consequences."[60] Senior had commented that the undereducated would undervalue education and would not demand the right quantity or quality; Mill repeated his idea: "it is but a poor education that associates ignorance with ignorance, and leaves them, if they care for knowledge, to grope their way to it without help, and to do without if they do not. What is wanted is, the means of making ignorance aware of itself, and able to profit by knowledge ... ."[61] Mill concurred with Senior and many of the other classicals that educational supply and demand presented unique difficulties since education was not "one of those marketable commodities which the interest of rival dealers can be depended upon for providing, in the quantity and quality required."[62] Therefore, Mill "urged strenuously the importance of having a provision for education, not dependent on the mere demand of the market, that is, on the knowledge and discernment of average parents, but calculated to establish and keep up a higher standard of instruction than is likely to be spontaneously demanded by the buyers of the article."[63] Mill placed very little trust in the ability of pauper parents to know what education was best for their children and he was certain that they had no concept of what was best for society as a whole.

In contrast, Herbert Spencer was not disturbed by the problems of parents too ignorant to judge quality education. Spencer thought that low income parents could watch the more knowledgeable higher income parents, and from them, learn to identify the schools which offered the kinds of education that suited their demand. Additionally, Spencer imagined that all the fuss over the inability of parents to select quality education would be short lived, because "the rising generation will better understand what good education is than their parents do, and their descendants will have a clearer conception of it still." He visualized a future society with a system of education that had evolved gradually through the free workings of supply and demand in a market system. He had witnessed some positive changes in the demand for education even within his own lifetime. Once again he emphasized "that society is a growth, and not a manufacture -- a thing that makes itself, and not a thing that can be artificially made, ... and we should see that ... this incompetence of the masses to distinguish good instruction from bad is being outgrown."[65]

Rather than anticipating the growth in good instruction over time and an increase in the demand for education, Marx and Engles expressed the futility of continuing attempts at education in a capitalistic system. They commented that "under existing conditions the division of labour replaces complex labour by simple labour, the labour of adults by that of children, the labour of men by that of women, the labour of independent workers by that of automations; that in proportion as modern industry develops, the education of the workers becomes unnecessary and impossible."[66] If the economic conditions which existed were maintained, Marx and Engles could foresee no reason for a future demand for education among the laboring class, as they would become more and more like appendages of the machines which they monitored.

Finally, Adam Smith, too, looked at the demand for education. He did not share James Mill's enthusiastic optimism, nor Nassau Senior's indecisive moderation, nor John Stuart Mill's unfettered pessimism. Like Herbert Spencer he championed the free market in educational provision and presumed that demand "not disturbed by any injudicious tampering" was most conducive to obtaining free market results. Legal or social schemes which guaranteed demand for an educational service would result in an educational supply of inferior quality, Smith reasoned. He cited two cases where this occurred: (1) when graduation is necessary for the practice of some profession, and (2) when charitable foundations or scholarships, exhibitions, and bursaries attach persons to certain schools.[67] Without these special circumstances, Smith remarked, after the ages of 12 or 13, children must be forced to attend school. This was untenable to him: "Force or restraint can scarce ever be necessary to carry on any part of education."[68]

Smith took both supply and demand elements of market equilibrium into account. If force had to be used to assure the demand for education, then it was obvious to Smith that the supply system of the service was at fault. He judged that instruction not taught in public schools, for instance fencing or dancing, was usually well taught. If it had *not* been provided efficiently, the teachers would have gone out of business. There was no need for compulsion for instruction in these subjects, because quality was guaranteed by the operation of the price system, Smith maintained.

Likewise Smith perceived that schools which were not public schools had to keep abreast of changes in consumer demand. These schools were encouraged to innovate, to try new methods and to include new subjects into their curricula in order to attract new pupils as well as to satisfy the needs of those students then in attendance. This was not the case with endowed schools which "have been the slowest in adapting ... (to) improvements, and the most adverse to permit any considerable change in the established plan of education." [69] Smith believed that the schools which were allowed to meet consumer demand following the tenets of the free market would prove to be the most successful. Furthermore, any aberation from free market provision would reduce the effectiveness of the school.

NOTES

1. Adam Smith, *An Inquiry into the Nature and Causes of the Wealth of Nations*, ed. Edwin Cannan (New York, 1937), p. 295.

2. Ibid., p. 16.

3. Ibid.

4. Adam Smith, *Lectures on Justice, Police, Revenue and Arms*, ed. Edwin Cannan (Oxford, 1896), p. 175.

5. Smith, *Wealth of Nations*, p. 103.

6. Smith, *Wealth of Nations*, p. 101.

7. Ibid.; also see Pierre N. V. Tu, "The Classical Economists and Education, *Kyklos*, Vol. 23, pp. 691-92, and "Adam Smith on Human Capital," by Joseph J. Spengler in *The American Economic Review*, Vol. 67 (1), pp. 32-36.

8. Smith, *Lectures*, p. 176.

9. Ibid.

10. Ibid.

11. Ibid.

12. Ibid.

13. David Ricardo, *The Works and Correspondence of David Ricardo*, Vol. I, p. 22.

14. Ibid., Vol. II, p. 115.

15. Jeremy Bentham, "Chrestomathia," *The Works of Jeremy Bentham*, ed. John Bowring (New York, 1962), p. 8.

16. Ibid., p. 20.

17. Ibid.

18. Jeremy Bentham, "Outline of a Work entitled Pauper Management Improved," *The Works of Jeremy Bentham*, ed. John Bowring (New York, 1962), p. 369.

19. Quoted in Brian Taylor, "A Note in Response to Itzen's "Bentham's 'Chrestomathia'," *Journal of the History of Ideas*, Vol. 43 (2), pp. 311.

20. J. B. Say, *A Treatise on Political Economy* (1821), (New York, 1964), p. 435.

21. Quoted in William Miller, "The Economics of Education in English Classical Economics," *Southern Economic Journal*, Vol. 32, p. 294.

22. John R. McCulloch, *The Principles of Political Economy*, 5th ed. (New York, 1965), p. 122.

23. Quoted in John MacCunn, *Six Radical Thinkers* (New York, 1964), p. 69.

24. John Stuart Mill, *Principles of Political Economy*, ed. William Ashley (Fairfield, 1976), p. 392.

25. Ibid., p. 392.

26. Ibid., pp. 107-8.

27. Ibid., pp. 386-7.

28. Nassau W. Senior, *Suggestions on Popular Education* (London, 1861), p. 86.

29. Nassau W. Senior, *An Outline of the Science of Political Economy* (New York, 1965), p. 69.

30. Quoted in Tu, p. 701.

31. Karl Marx and Friedrich Engles, *Manifesto of the Communist Party* (Moscow, 1977), p. 70.

32. Ibid., p. 68.

33. Ibid., p. 70.

34. Karl Marx and Friedrich Engles, *Collected Works* (New York, 1975), Vol. IV, pp. 253-54.

35. Ibid.

36. Henry Fawcett, *Pauperism: Its Causes and Remedies* (New York, 1871), p. 125.

37. Ibid., p. 129.

38. A. C. O. Ellis, "Influences on School Attendance in Victorian England," *British Journal of Educational Studies*, Vol. 21 (3), p. 313.

39. Ibid., p. 317.

40. Smith, *Wealth of Nations*, p. 737.

41. Smith, *Lectures*, p. 256.

42. Ibid.

43. Ibid., p. 257.

44. Ibid.

45. Nassau Senior, *Industrial Efficiency and Social Economy*, ed. S. Leon Levy (New York, 1928), p. 334.

46. Senior, *An Outline*, p. 207.

47. Senior, *Industrial Efficiency*, p. 333.

48. Ibid., p. 334.

49. Ibid., p. 339.

50. Ibid.

51. Herbert Spencer, *Social Statics* (New York, 1954), p. 295.

52. Ibid.

53. A. C. O. Ellis explores this thoroughly in his article on school attendance.

54. See: Lawrence Stone, "Literacy and Education in England 1640-1900," *Past and Present*, No. 42, pp. 67-139 and David Mitch, "The Spread of Literacy in Nineteenth-Century England," *The Journal of Economic History*, Vol. 43 (1), pp. 287-88 and J. H. Plumb, "The New World of Children in Eighteenth-Century England, *Past and Present*, No. 67, pp. 64-93.

55. Mitch, p. 288.

56. Quoted in E. G. West, "Tom Paine's Voucher Scheme for Public Education," *Southern Economic Journal*, Vol. 33 (3), p. 379.

57. Senior, *Industrial Efficiency*, p. 335.

58. Ibid.

59. Ibid.

60. John Stuart Mill, *On Liberty*, ed. Currin V. Shields (New York, 1956), pp. 100-101.

61. John Stuart Mill, *Considerations on Representative Government*, (Southbend, Indiana, 1962), p. 305.

62. Quoted in Edward Alexander, *Matthew Arnold and John Stuart Mill* (New York, 1965), p. 222.

63. Ibid., p. 222.

64. Spencer, *Social Statics*, p. 302.

65. Ibid.

66. Marx and Engles, *Collected Works*, Vol. VIII, p. 260.

67. Smith, *Wealth of Nations*, p. 719.

68. Ibid., p. 720.

69. Ibid., p. 727.

CHAPTER V

EDUCATIONAL SUPPLY: OBSERVATIONS
FROM THE CLASSICAL ECONOMISTS

INTRODUCTION

Before 1850, many countries relied on a system of educational supply organized around voluntary contributions, modest fees for instruction, and/or some small measure of state financial aid. For example, in 1765 the grammar school that Adam Smith attended was supported by fees levied upon the subjects selected by the pupil or his parents. "English by itself" cost one shilling and sixpence per quarter while "English writing and vulgar arithmetic with one hour writing daily" cost two shillings; "Latin and Greek or Greek verse" could be had for five shillings per quarter and "Decimal arithmetic, mensuration, trigonometry and algebra" sold for three shillings. "Church music (on occasion)" was "gratis." The existence of such an array of services at a variety of prices caused Robert Lowe to observe: "In Scotland they sell education like a grocer sells figs."[1]

In France in the early 1800s, data indicate that there was a school in each town, although student fees were but a small measure of total school financing.[2] The typical method of maintaining a French school was through the allocation of a fixed yearly salary for the teacher out of local revenues. This salary was supplemented by a fee assessed on the families of the children attending school. Only rarely was the instructor's recompense from the town set so high as to make the student fees unnecessary. Usually, the teacher was obliged to teach a certain number of indigent children without charge.[3]

Prior to the 1830s, most of the teachers in France relied on an association with the parish priest for part of their livelihood. These "lay clerics" were generally semiliterate, hired more for their ability to perform services for the church than for their aptitude for instruction. After 1830, however, there was a growing movement to foster teacher training in France through normal schools. The graduates of these institutions rejected the usual position of clerical subordinate and refused to perform such normally accepted tutorial duties as sweeping the church and maintaining the cemetery.[4] This professional stance did not help their remuneration, however, and throughout the early decades of the 1800s, teacher's salaries were so exceptionally low that they were forced to moonlight to meet their expenses. Many preferred this to subservience to the parish priest even though it often meant a stint as a migratory agricultural worker.

69

After 1850, the demand for the services of teachers in France began to rise, and with it, teacher pay and prestige. With the passage of the French compulsory education laws, problems of truancy and punctuality diminished considerably. Additionally, free adult education classes were offered by the school teachers to demonstrate directly to parents the usefulness of education. The teachers considered these classes their best form of advertisement and they "subsidized them by teaching without remuneration and even by paying out of their own pockets the cost of heating and lighting ... at night."[5] These methods were so successful that by the 1870s parents had begun to feel differently about sending their children to school; parents even admitted feeling guilty if their children failed to attend their lessons. With the stronger demand for education, by the end of the century, teachers' salaries had risen to be comparable to those of artisans and were significantly higher than most lower class occupations.[6] A final sign of long term stability among the teaching profession in France was that turnover rates for teachers had begun to decline; this indicated that teaching was beginning to be considered a practicable occupation.

In Germany of the early 1800s, the financial plight of the teacher was less severe than in France. More communal resources were earmarked for school maintenance in the German states and, although much of the teacher's payment was in kind or in land, each small town could easily afford to have an instructor. The size of the teacher's cash salary was variable, based upon "the fiscal situation of the town budget and the political opinion of the town council."[7] It is interesting that sometimes the fixed part of the teacher's salary was not a direct grant from the state, but a voluntary contribution made to either the Catholic or Evangelical Ministry, by individuals and redistributed to the local schools.[8]

If financially the German teacher were more secure, intellectually, he was at least equal to his French counterpart. An 1802 study found incompetent teachers, ungraded schools in bad repair, little instruction in reading and writing but much emphasis on religion. One social commentator of the time recorded this job description for a German teacher: "If he could read but poorly, sing the best-known church hymns, repeat the five articles of the smaller Lutheran catechism, and could write, then he possessed all the qualities necessary for a good teacher, and more was not required of him."[9] However, as in France, changing times necessitated an upgrading of the German teaching corps.

The English educational supply before 1860 was a combination of church related schools, charity schools, Dame schools, and Sunday schools. The earliest education legislation in England provided funds to aid established schools recondition their physical facilities. Supplementing the monies from the state was a tuition charge which was customary throughout the nineteenth century.

One pervasive type of school in England during the 1800s was the endowed institution. An example of a typical endowed charity school was the Old Swinford Hospital School; its history was illustrative of the changes which the successful endowed school was forced to make to survive.[10] In 1667, Thomas Foley decided to use his inherited wealth in a very social minded way: he established a school for the sons of poor but honest rural parents. Of the sixty students enrolled, fourteen would be "choice" and forty-six would come from the "parish." The school's trustees selected the parish boys who had to be "not less than seven nor more than ten years of age, free from infection, sores or lameness, and members of the Church of England." An additional condition was that the student's family must not have accepted any prior parish relief. Upon completion of the required course of study (typically at age fourteen) the student was apprenticed to a trade or industry as stipulated by the founder's will.

During the 1800s Old Swinford Hospital School experienced a period of growth in the demand for its services. The number of students was raised and more "air and exercise" were incorporated into the program. The curriculum concentrated on the three R's to prepare pupils for their industrial or commercial apprenticeships. Even after graduation, the careers of the former students were monitored which allowed the school's management to keep abreast of the educational needs of the community.

However by the 1870s the ability of the school to meet the founder's wishes faded as apprenticeships disappeared and new career opportunities beckoned. In the early years of the twentieth century, the educational system which Thomas Foley had envisioned was all but extinct; it was impossible to carry out his desire to send students into apprenticeship programs following their education. Nevertheless, for over one hundred years Old Swinford Hospital School had provided an adequate supply of workers to the trades and industries of its region. As many other endowed institutions, Old Swinford Hospital School tried to fulfill the mission identified for it when it was created. When it could continue to do so, it remained in operation, but when the environment had changed so radically that these outdated mandates were no longer possible to achieve, the endowed school's doors were closed.

The classicals had a variety of opinions on basic educational supply. They all recognized the unique supply problems that

71

education created. Some thought that free market provision would be the best solution; some felt that only other types of educational supply could meet the needs of a growing society. The thoughts of the classical political economists generally differed in relation to specialized training. Since this good would bring specific returns to those who consumed it, the free market price could be used to determine the supply of technical education. However, some classicals did not agree with this conclusion, maintaining that true technical education was a social good, and should be supplied as such. Finally, the classicals were eager to express their thoughts on university education. Many of them were products of the university system and willingly wrote of suggestions for its reform.

OBSERVATIONS ON CLASSICAL SUPPLY

Smith commented on the supply of education in Britain in the 1700s. He held the endowment system in disfavor because he thought that it reduced the level of effort required of teachers. He wrote, "The endowments of schools and colleges have necessarily diminished more or less the necessity of application in the teachers."[11] This occurred because the teachers' "subsistence, so far as it arises from their salaries, is evidently derived from a fund altogether independent of their success and reputation in their particular professions."[12] Therefore, if pay were not tied to effort, Smith reasoned, the teachers would be encouraged to work as little as possible. Smith was quick to point out the effects of endowments on privately funded education. He recognized that the salaries paid in the two institutions could never be competitive. Smith described the impossible condition of the private teacher as similar to "a merchant who attempts to trade without a bounty in competition with those who trade with a considerable one." Futilely trying to compete in such a situation would lead to "poverty and beggary at least, if not bankruptcy and ruin."[13] Smith concluded that because of endowments, it is "almost impossible to have any good private" teachers and he predicted few good teachers in endowed schools, as well.[14]

Smith also disapproved of endowed schools for their stubborn adherence to the wishes of the founders of the institutions. In this instance, Smith even *called* for state action. He thought that the state had the right to ensure that all endowments were managed to promote the social good, rather than to perpetuate the outdated aims of those persons who had originally funded the school decades or centuries before.[15]

Fifty years after Smith had disparaged endowments, John Stuart Mill reflected that much still remained to be done to bring endowed schools into the mainstream of modern educational

72

thinking. Mill supported the idea that it was meritorious to leave property for "founding a place of education;" but he thought the act ceased to be laudable when the benefactor "dictates, for ever, what doctrines should be taught." Mill had observed needed changes in the supply of education within his own lifetime and decided that, "It being impossible that anyone should know what doctrines will be fit to be taught after he has been dead for centuries, the law ought not to give effect to such dispositions of property, unless subject to perpetual revision (after a certain interval has elapsed) of a fitting authority."[16] Mill echoed Smith's suggestion of state action.

Herbert Spencer concurred with Mill. Writing about fifty years after Mill, he called endowed institutions "places of intellectual stagnation." He viewed Oxford and Eton as suppressors of knowledge and considered these the last places where anyone should look for educational improvements or advances in learning. According to Spencer, "Richly endowed, strengthened by their *prestige*, and by the bias given to those they have brought up, our colleges, public schools, and other kindred schools early founded, useful as they once were, have long been enormous impediments to a higher education. By subsidizing the old, they have starved the new ... ."[17] Tradition forced these traditional places of learning into supplying outmoded education.

Smith, Mill, and then Spencer had railed against the endowed schools accusing them of lagging behind the educational needs of the times, as well as fostering low quality teaching. They concentrated the blame for this on the fact that there was no connection between reward and results. The endowed schools would continue to be funded no matter how lethargic their teachers or how irrelevant their courses as long as they met with the founder's conditions. Nevertheless, a century of negative classical opinion about these endowed institutions had not apparently altered their way of operating to any degree. The problems which Smith perceived in the late 1700s were entrenched in the system by the end of the 1800s.

To discourage teacher lethargy and irrelevant subjects in schools that were not endowed, Smith demanded that the teachers be recompensed in some way from honoraries or small fees from pupils, thereby making the instructor financially dependent on his pupils. This Smith hoped would force the teacher to maintain his professional integrity: "Reputation in his profession is still of some importance to him, and he still has some dependency upon the affection, gratitude and favorable report of those who have attended his instructions."[18] Smith continued that the natural way to gain student affections was by "deserving them, that is, by the abilities and diligence with which he discharges every part of his duty."[19] In sum, Smith relied once again on operations of the free market, believing that direct rewards in education would provide quality teachers.

Malthus and McCulloch reiterated Smith's ideas on student fees. Malthus thought that "the school master would ... have a stronger interest to increase the number of his pupils" if he were paid per head.[20] Presumably the teacher would be encouraged to make the supply of his service more desirable and would try to please his "customers" so that he could continue his livelihood and, becoming accomplished in his endeavors, make a nice profit from it. McCulloch followed this line of thought with the idea that student fees would "secure the constant attendance of a person who shall be able to instruct the young, and who shall have the strongest interest to perfect himself in his business, and to attract the greatest number of scholars to his school."[21] McCulloch, as others of his time, regarded those who held sine-cures as mere "functionaries" who neglected their business and "consider it as drudgery only to be avoided" while they collect their pay.[22] The teacher whose payment was not tied to results would adopt a similar attitude, McCulloch predicted.

Some educational thinkers had suggested that the careful observation of teachers by a supervisory staff would be one way of forcing them to provide better instruction. Smith countered that supervision would only compel teachers to comply with quantity constraints but would not affect lecture quality. Moreover, Smith envisioned this supervisory body as just an additional bureaucratic layer and, like so many other government bodies, would become "plagued by the insolence of office" and would "ensure or deprive wantonly" thereby degrading the teachers into obsequious postures."[23] Supervision of teachers would be a poor substitute for direct market interaction between the teachers and their pupils, Smith maintained.

As much as Smith desired a free market solution to the educational problem, he did not think of education as just any other type of market good. He had written of the microeconomic and macroeconomic effects which education promised to provide for society, especially for the poor. But he recognized the difficulty of furnishing education for the poor in a system which depended upon the generation of profit to motivate supply. Smith reasoned that since the business of providing education to the laboring classes was one in which profit was small or non-existent, modern governments must "take great pains" to prevent "the almost entire corruption and degeneracy of the great body of people."[24] Nevertheless, whatever the scheme for pauper education selected, Smith maintained that it would be preferable to have at least some of the teacher's compensation covered by fees from students no matter how small a portion of the payment this might be.

74

During the late eighteenth century, voluntary contributions, together with small student fees, were an important part of the funding of English education. Early in the nineteenth century, James Mill had little doubt that if the Lancasterian methods were used, the cost of providing education to "the poor of two or more villages in one school" could be reduced to such a trifle, that for each district it is not surely too much to hope that in voluntary contributions (financing) might be found."[25] Philanthropic support for education was the backbone of the early English educational experience, especially when the numbers of students were still "reasonably" small.

Jeremy Bentham, entrepreneur par excellence, advocated two schemes for predominantly privately sponsored education. The initial funding for each scheme was to be through subscription, but each system was designed for a different income group. The first, Chrestomathia, was intended for those who could afford to pay for the cost of their education; the second, the National Charity Company, was established to educate the poor through a private enterprise rather than in the workhouse. In many ways, the plan for Chrestomathia was typical of the middle class schools of that era. First, a criterion for admission was that the students be "children whose domestic circumstances and local situation concur in putting it in their power to avail themselves of the proffered services."[26] However, Bentham did suggest the possibility of charitable wealthy sponsors paying the tuition for children of insufficient means. Second, there was an attempt at a broadened curriculum which included practical, as well as theoretic instruction to prepare the Chrestomathic students for their future roles in society. Meticulously, Bentham justified and explained every subject to be taught in the school.[27] In Bentham's school a noteworthy omission from the usual curriculum was religious training.[28] Although this neutral religious position would cause the project endless difficulties, Bentham held firm to his belief that religious instruction would "naturally" be furnished in the home and had no place in the formal classroom.

The ultimate control of Chrestomathia would be in the hands of the contributors-owners. They would have the right to visit the school and to make recommendations for its improvement. Bentham insisted that not only through financial help, but also through wise guidance, the subscribers would be providing the diffusion of useful knowledge to the children of the middle class. He also concluded that the wealthy subscribers who sponsored children of families who could not afford the school fees were performing a public charity as well.

Bentham's second plan concerning the supply of education was unique. Since Chrestomathia was planned essentially for the middle class, a separate educational system was necessary to

75

reach the multitudinous poor. The National Charity Company was Bentham's idea for a scheme that would make profit from the operation of "Industry Houses" for paupers. The poor would work as well as learn in this environment.

The most important benefit to education which Bentham anticipated from this novel type of educational supply was the absence of direct government involvement. First, Bentham hoped that problems of favoritism which occurred in the awarding of educational appointments and governmental contracts would disappear under the National Charity Company educational plan. He envisioned a lessening of the "jealousy of *influence*" and of the inefficiencies occurring when real or even imagined cases of nepotism were part of the working environment. Second, Bentham remarked that there would be the "benefit of a distinct *check* from the superintending power of government."[29] He could foresee no positive results from the imposition of a supervisory level of government bureaucrats. Bentham, as Smith, believed in general that the less government involvement in any process, including education, the better. Finally, as in Chrestomathia, the National Charity Company owners would exercise great influence over the students who attended its schools. However, in Bentham's words, this promise seemed almost ominous: "The influence of the schoolmaster on the conduct of the pupil in ordinary life, is nothing compared with the influence exercised by the company over these its wards."[30]

David Ricardo was eager to become a supporter of Chrestomathia. Although the place of education in his economic thinking was far from clear, in his personal life he was firmly convinced of the need for a well ordered supply of education in the basic skills. He financed out of his own pocket the construction and maintenance of a school for the poor on his estate at Gatcomb. Furthermore, he pledged two hundred pounds to Bentham's Chrestomathia. Adhering to the principle of voluntary contributions to support education, he "willingly" contributed fifty pounds to an infant day school proposed by Robert Owen for the children of workers at one of Owen's factories.

Ricardo faced conflicting beliefs since on the one hand he valued pauper education and on the other hand he feared the repercussions from an increase in aid to the poor. The results of the Poor Law legislation discouraged Ricardo and he felt that any type of payment which reduced parental responsibility was a disillusionment to those very person which it was intended to help. With his check for Owen's proposed day school, Ricardo stipulated that his contribution was given with the clear understanding that the school "take care of or only educate the children that are admitted to this institution."[31] He plainly reiterated that "if it is part of the plan ... to feed as well as to take care of and educate the children of three years of age and upwards, belonging to the poor, I see the most serious objections to the plan." [32] In Ricardo's thinking, private funding could easily supply the educational needs of the middle and working classes. Regarding the education of the poor, he was certain that some external public action was necessary, but was equally determined that this action be kept to a minimum.

Herbert Spencer also firmly believed in the social benefits from greater individual parental responsibility. In some ways, Spencer sounded very much like James Mill when Mill made his case for domestic education. Spencer contrasted the work of the hired teacher to that of the parent-teacher:

> When the minds of children are no longer stunted and deformed by the mechanical lessons of stupid teachers, ... when the earlier stages of education passed through in the domestic circle have come to yield ... daily occasions for the strengthening of sympathy, intellectual and moral, then will the latter days of life be smoothed by a greater filial care, reciprocating the greater parental care bestowed in earlier life. [33]

Government supplied education had grown dramatically by the time Spencer wrote. He dreaded the content of the "mechanical lessons of stupid teachers," lessons which precluded diversity of thought or opinion. Moreover, Spencer's estimation of government was very low: he believed that no government could be "competent to say what education should be, either in matter, manner, or order." [34] Spencer not only challenged government's right to determine educational supply but he also contested "its right to impose its system of culture upon the citizen, so that under penalty for disobedience his children may be moulded after its approved pattern." [35]

Spencer reasoned that government as the provider of education would *necessarily* omit subjects which cause students to question their political economic system. Government adhered to things that confirm the status quo, not things which threatened to change it, Spencer maintained: "Much thinking being held at variance with good citizenship, the teaching of metaphysics, political economy, and the like is discouraged." [36] However detrimental the lack of these subjects, more damning, according to Spencer, would be the omission of the subjects which resulted in "character making." Since a state would never recognize "character making" as the aim of its educational system, Spencer thought, it would therefore neglect to provide the most necessary instruction of all. [37]

Wilhelm von Humboldt protested state supply of education because of its uniform treatment of individuals. Humboldt stressed the fact that national education was necessarily structured since "it presupposes the selection and appointment of some particular instructor (and) must always promote a definite form of development." He continued, "if there is one thing more than another which absolutely requires free activity on the part of the individual, it is precisely education."[38] The state appeared not to recognize this fact since within a state system of educational supply there were no allowances for exceptions.

Moreover, the presence of the state in education led to mediocrity, Humboldt deduced. National education could not be directed toward the "encouragement of any particular virtue or disposition" or toward any particular type of "character making." The best that it could possibly do was to create a state of "balance,"

> ... since balance is most conducive to the peace and quiet that the state is zealously seeking to establish. But such efforts ... either produce a standstill in progress or a lack of energy, whereas the pursuit of individual traits and talents made possible by private education produces, quite another balance, one brought about itself, and without the sacrifice of energy.[39]

Only education which was maintained in its "most lively and vigorous form" would benefit students in their later years, he averred.

Humboldt relied on Smithian reasoning when he presumed that the profit motive would encourage better teaching, which would in time result in a greater demand for education. He noticed that "teachers educate themselves better when their fortunes depend on their own efforts, than when their chances of promotion rest on what they are led to expect from the state."[40] If teachers could be inspired to produce good quality instruction through the search for profit, "there would ... be no want of ... private educational establishments which are so useful and indispensable."[41] Finally, Humboldt foretold of the emergence of "careful family training." As Smith and James Mill, he declared that domestic education was the foundation of a thorough and efficient educational supply system.

Bastiat was confused about the educational standards which would be adopted under a system of state provided educational supply. He did not object to consistently applied educational standards as long as they were the best that could be devised. Clearly he explained, "if people could agree on the best possible kind of education, in regard to both content and method, a uniform system of public instruction would be preferable, since error would, in that case, be necessarily excluded by law."[42] He continued, "but as long as such a criterion has not been found, as long as the legislator and the Minister of Public Education do not carry on their persons an unquestionable sign of infallibility," the chance for finding a bench mark for educational excellence was small in a governmentally controlled environment.[43] Bastiat considered that only "if room is left for diversity, trial and error, experimentation, and individual efforts guided by a self-regarding *interest in the outcome*," could there be the possibility of discovering the best educational scheme.[44] The worst conditions for educational improvement occurred "in a uniform system of education established by decree, for in such a system error is permanent, universal, and irremediable ... ."[45] Bastiat used the educational experience in Napoleonic France as an example of a completely regulated educational environment.

Bastiat judged that part of the state's inability to supply quality educational services was due to the very nature of public servants. Of the civil servant, he opined: "The public official ... is deprived of the stimulus that urges us on to progress."[46] As teachers and school administrators moved from the private enterprise system into the public domain, Bastiat predicted that they would "lose momentum, at least to some degree, and become sterile, not to (their own) detriment ... (their pay does not change,) but to the detriment of the whole community."[47] Bastiat was in the company of Smith, Malthus and McCulloch when he criticized the efforts of government employees.

John Stuart Mill flatly rejected Bastiat's belief in the power of nongovernmentally supplied education to efficiently meet the needs of the future of society. He thought little of the voluntary principle of education and held "that even in quantity it is, and is likely to remain, altogether insufficient, while in quality, though with some slight tendency to improvement, it is never good except by some rare accident, and generally so bad as to be little more than nominal."[48] Unlike his classical predecessors, Mill took a long run view of universal education and found that no permanent, country-wide, uniform system of instruction could be possible merely through philanthropic efforts.

Mill's opinion of the teacher who taught under a privately sponsored educational plan was equally low. Mill was specific: "In the first place, he has a direct pecuniary interest in neglecting all studies not cared for by the general public, or by the section of it from whom he hopes for patronage." If he does attempt to teach anything, Mill continued, he aims "at a mere appearance of proficiency" not "at the reality." The reason why the teacher can escape his duty, Mill felt, was because there was

79

no examination of the pupils to see what, if anything, they had been taught. Mill held parents as unreliable judges of quality education since "many ... know little of what is taught at schools, or have forgotten what they knew; many of whom do not test their child's knowledge by a single question, it being enough for them that he has been at what is called a respectable school." Mill ended this discussion with a clear condemnation of the voluntary principle: "These are not the abuses, but the natural fruits, of the trading principle in education." [49]

Interestingly, in opposition to J. S. Mill's opinion that the voluntary principle could not work, Nassau Senior and the New-castle Commission reported in 1861 that there were over two and a half million children attending school, ninety-five percent of the school age population. This account indicated that the voluntary principle of school supply had indeed been successful, at least as successful as schemes in other European countries, even those where compulsory state education was legislated. But in line with one objection of John Stuart Mill, Senior's chief difficulty lay with school quality rather than school quantity. He perceived that there were no controls over teacher qualifications and that, with free selection, parents often chose the wrong schools for the wrong reasons. Many parents rejected quality schools (such as those proposed by Jeremy Bentham) because they considered them ordinary "or their boy had been punished there, or he is required to be clean, or to be regular, or the private school is half a street nearer, or is kept by a friend, or by someone who will submit his teaching to their dictation." [50] Senior decided that free choice in schooling could be dangerous, if parents could not make good choices. John Stuart Mill and Nassau Senior were the most vocal classicists on this idea.

Henry Sidgwick did not feel as strongly as some of the other classical economists that parental discretion was a major fault with the provision of educational supply on a free market basis. Sidg-wick was solidly behind the use of voluntary contributions to increase the well-being of society. He considered how much had been done in the past toward raising the level of education by the "spontaneous association of the persons primarily concerned or the philanthropic efforts of other individuals." [51] Sidgwick went so far as to give private initiative most of the credit for the gains in civilization which had been achieved: "the promotion of education and culture and the cure of diseases, have been largely provided for in modern civilized communities by the voluntary contributions of individuals; partly by donations, partly by bequests." [52] The record of individuals freely giving needed funds to promote social advance had been more than sufficient to meet social problems in the past, Sidgwick asserted.

Sidgwick did not think that the kindly nature of people

would change to upset the adequacy of private provision: "the genuine philanthropists among (us) are keenly desirous to give to others less fortunate." But he wondered if voluntary contributions could furnish enough funds for "the general and technical education required for economic efficiency."[53] A growing economy demanded basic education of all its citizens and industrial sophistication required specific training in technological skills. Sidgwick doubted that voluntary funds could cover these advanced educational needs. He wrote also that fundamental attitudes in society toward what was "essential" education was changing: "I might remind you of the resolution recently passed at a Socialistic Congress, that University education should be effectively open to all classes of the community, from the highest to the lowest; for even an extravagance of this kind is a straw that shows how strongly the current of opinion is flowing."[54] Sidgwick could see that the majority of the population was no longer content with living lives of barely educated laborers; in fact, he knew that "the widespread determination to aim, even in elementary teaching, at something more than the *minimum* required for economic efficiency" was fast becoming a popular sentiment. [55]

In the rapidly changing social and economic thinking of the late nineteenth century, universal education was viewed as a prerequisite to individual and societal welfare. Sidgwick detected some very practical problems with trying to supply this education under free market rules. Smith had commented on the small or nonexistent profit to be made directly from educational supply. Sidgwick considered a "loan" arrangement whereby one individual would furnish the funds for another's education "with the view of being repaid out of the salary of the labourers educated." [56] Sidgwick concluded that "it would not be profitable for anyone else to provide the money" because there were two problems associated with this repayment: (1) "the jural difficulty of making contracts with children," and (2) "the interest required to compensate for the trouble and risk of the deferred payments would be practically prohibitive."[57] Because of these complexities, Sidgwick suggested that the community could provide basic education and even "technical and professional education at a cheap rate, ... when it would not be profitable for any private individual to do this."[58]

Sidgwick was reluctant to resort to government help for solutions to the problems which were emerging in a changing economy. This was obvious in his warning: "It does not of course follow that wherever *laissez-faire* falls short, government interference is expedient; since the inevitable drawbacks and disadvantages of the latter may, in a particular case, be worse then the shortcomings of private industry."[59] Nevertheless, the sticky legal problems of contracts with juveniles, the lack of adequate return to private investors, and the conspicuous need for universal and technical education were strong reasons to seek government involvement in educational supply, Sidgwick judged.

APPRENTICESHIPS AND TECHNICAL TRAINING

Henry Sidgwick commented on the possibility of government provision of "technical education at a cheap rate." Yet the idea of government activity in providing technological expertise was not new. "Schools of Industry" had their humble beginnings as early as 1787 when a Mrs. Trimmer formed a spinning school; she then quickly demanded parish aid for her efforts.[60] Many reasoned that the only way to disseminate the badly needed technical training rapidly was through the intervention of government. This became a hotly debated topic for at least one hundred years.

Government intervention into monitoring the quality of workmanship dates back to the time of the apprenticeship laws. Adam Smith had several comments on the subject of apprenticeship legislation and the need for the state in technical training.[61] First, he judged that long apprenticeships resulted in an aversion to work since the apprentice had to commit so much time to his occupation before receiving any substantial rewards. By the time a man was made a craftsman, he may have already become tired of his craft. Second, Smith considered most of these long apprenticeships totally unnecessary to the learning process. Without regulations, the workmen themselves could be trained to produce quality products in a much shorter length of time. Smith described the futility of state interference in skills training: "It was imagined that the cause of so much bad cloth was that the weaver had not been properly educated, and therefore they made a statute that he should serve a seven years apprenticeship before he pretended to make any. But this is by no means a sufficient security against bad cloth ... [62]." Smith deduced that the free market would provide high returns to quality products which would reflect the training of their producers. Consequently, government involvement could only frustrate a naturally simple solution. However, it was not until a quarter of a century after Smith's death when the Elizabethan Statute of Artificers was repealed, that this interference with trade education was finally removed.[63]

James Mill could recall from memory the results of state involvement in apprenticeship training. His disfavor with the state program was clear cut: "Whether these apprenticeships, as they have hitherto been managed, have been good instruments of education, is a question of importance, about which there is now among enlightened men, hardly any diversity of opinion."[64] Mill continued: "When the legislature undertakes to do for every man what every man had abundant motives to do for himself, and better means than the legislature, the legislature takes on a very unnecessary and commonly not very innocent trouble."[65]   Mill's statement could apply equally to all kinds of state interference as well as to technical training and apprenticeship programs.   Adam Smith and James Mill both objected strongly to government interruption of the supply of labor to specific markets.

In contrast Friedrich Engles accepted the notion that state education was essential to social development.   Furthermore he had confidence in his discovery of a type of education that he felt was philosophically attuned to the needs of a changing society.   Engles praised "Socialist institutes" where the students "received a purely proletarian education, free from all the influences of the bourgeoisie."   He was particularly encouraged by the fact that these technical schools were often established by and for the working men.   Workers were bored with the education offered to them by the bourgeoisie, education which they considered "tame, flabby, subservient to the ruling politics and religion."[66]   To the worker, this kind of learning was "merely a constant sermon upon quiet obedience, passivity, and resignation to his fate."[67]   Engles knew that the workers hungered for "solid education" and he happily reported the early success of these workers' schools: German workers were even getting more knowledge than the "cultivated" bourgeoisie.

Engles suspected that the bourgeoisie would not remain ignorant of the power that technical education gave to the workers.   Before long, the middle classes were branding workers' schools as "very dangerous" and were rapidly successful "in withdrawing several such institutes, Mechanics Institutes, from proletarian influences."[68]   Engles supposed that these schools would be replaced, to the workers' dismay, by bourgeoisie schools which would be "organs for the dissemination of the sciences useful to the bourgeoisie."   Here the worker would be taught only what he had to know to serve the capitalist boss.   Ironically, by frustrating the success of the one type of educational institution that could ease the worker into a new classless society, Engles wrote, the bourgeoisie was condemning itself to a radical social alternative.

As Engles, Marx, too, was disenchanted with the technical education pressed upon the workers of his day.   In a series of "lectures on Political Economy to the German Workers Society" given in 1847, he discussed a "suggestion, very popular with the bourgeoisie, ... *education*, especially comprehensive *industrial education*."[69]   Marx criticized this proposed educational plan on four counts: (1) labor replaced by machinery did not need education, (2) school laws were meaningless when children were still employed running the machines of the factory, (3) education had no positive effect on wages because even the educated worker became unemployed through the growing use of machinery; the skilled unemployed then competed for the scarce remaining jobs by offering their services at reduced rates. Marx's final point was reminiscent of Engles: technical training was, in fact, merely more bourgeois moral indoctrination. At this time in his career, Marx deemed the technological education being proffered to the worker as virtually meaningless to society's economic advance.[70] Marx and Engles thought that in the educational realm, as well as in society as a whole, the time was ripe for change.

UNIVERSITY EDUCATION

Although the classical writers concentrated heavily on basic education in much of their writing on education, they could not let higher education and the university system pass without comment. Postsecondary educational opportunities of the day certainly called for critical observation. The universities of Britain were not designed to furnish the student with learning useful in earning a living. If the student were the son of an entrepreneur and was guaranteed entrance into the family firm upon graduation, little of the knowledge that he acquired at the university would be helpful in his career. Rather, the education in the public school and in the university was expected to instill in the student the tastes and habits of a way of life: that of the gentry or that of the aristocracy. Additionally, students and their parents steeped in the values of traditional education were careful not to demand any substantive change in university education. It was not surprising that Cambridge had no chemistry laboratory until 1877 and no engineering lab until 1894.[71]

Adam Smith did not hesitate to condemn what he had observed in the universities of his day. He openly criticized the British university system: "In the University of Oxford, the greater part of the public professors have, for these many years, given up altogether the pretense of teaching."[72] He likened university graduates to apprentices who had served their legal apprenticeships – they had merely served their time. With unusual vituperation Smith called the English institutions of higher learning "sanctuaries in which exploded systems and obsolete prejudices found shelter and protection, after they had been hunted out of every corner of the world."[73] Harboring these feelings, few were amazed that Smith left Oxford even before his scholarship had expired.

Smith identified another example of a shoddy university practice – the Grand Tour. Smith accused the universities of engaging in fraud when they sent students abroad to round out their education. He penned in scathing tones: "Nothing but the discredit into which universities are allowing themselves to fall could ever have brought into repute so very absurd a practice as that of traveling at this early period of life."[74] Smith accused the universities of shirking their responsibility of providing sound and relevant instruction by sending their students away to acquire knowledge as best they could.

Jeremy Bentham was personally distressed by the poor quality instruction he found at Queen's College. Attending in 1760 at the age of thirteen, he was compelled to read Cicero's speeches and the Greek testament. He was intensely disappointed with this assignment since he had already memorized all of Cicero and could recite it by heart. He also claimed to have mastered the Greek testament years before.[74]

John Stuart Mill who did not attend any university did have some recommendations for the general university curriculum. Universities should "keep alive philosophy," while teaching students to think for themselves. More specifically, the universities should avoid association with the "huckstering virtues." Mill thought that universities should show the student the foundations of knowledge and the means of appreciating life. In opposition to the movement that universities should be path-breakers in fostering commercial advance, Mill wrote, "the empirical knowledge which the world demands, which is the stock in trade of money-getting life, we would leave the world to provide for itself ... ."[76]

As unsettled as the university situation was in Britain, in France conditions were decidedly worse. After the French Revolution of 1789, the twenty-two universities which had formed the nucleus of higher education in France were abolished. Presumably this was a small loss, since it was reported that there was little learning occurring in any of them.[77] In 1806, to fill the void left by the closed universities, Napoleon created a monopoly university.

Claude Frederic Bastiat's strongest argument against state interference in education was directed against Napoleon's monopoly university. Only the bureaucratic university corps was permitted to confer academic degrees. This particularly annoyed Bastiat who was convinced that places of education should be changeable because education was "a treasure that is refined and increased every day" and was passed on from generation to generation.[78] Since the French university system had "the threefold inconvenience of making education *uniform*, of imposing upon it the *most disastrous administration*, and then making it flexible: the influence of this kind of education would be felt throughout the decades, he wrote.[79] Internally, as well as externally, the university system of France was out of touch with modern educational needs. The traditional classical educational curriculum was at the heart of the French educational plan. Bastiat queried: "Is Latin a necessary means for the acquisition of knowledge? Can religion, physics, chemistry, psysiology, history, law, ethics, industrial technology, or social science be learned from the writings left to us by the Romans:"[80] He mused, "If only the knowledge required for the bachelor's degree still bore some relation to the needs and interests of our age."[81] Frenchmen had to wait many years before Bastiat's appeal for reforms in higher education was begun.

As in France, German higher education was under complete control of the government but the philosophical emphasis of German education was dramatically different from the French experience. German control of higher education was all pervasive; the German government had the final say even in faculty appointments. Nevertheless, free market elements still were employed to affect the quality of teaching. Faculty income was composed of two parts: a state stipend, and supplemental payments to the faculty by the students.[82] Using the Smithian idea of payments by reward and direct payment between pupils and their teachers, the Germans were able to build a system of higher education that was the envy of all Europe.

Napoleon indirectly brought about the formation of the new German university system. In 1806 the University of Berlin was established to replace the universities at Jena and Halle which had been closed by the Napoleonic invasion. This institution became the model for all other universities in the system. The person singled out to oversee the beginnings of the University of Berlin was Wilhelm von Humboldt. He instigated basic reforms which were subsequently adopted by universities throughout the world. The two basic principles which Humboldt believed would result in a strong learning environment in the university were (1) to appoint the best intellects available, and (2) to give them freedom to carry on their research.[83] But he recognized that the university depended upon the secondary schools for the quality of its incoming students. So he reorganized the system of secondary schools so that its lines into the university system were obvious and direct. Anyone who had successfully completed the final examination of a Gymnasium (secondary school) had the right to enter and study at the university. This increased the demand for quality in the secondary schools while assuring a steady supply of pupils to the university. Finally, Humboldt admitted that "the nature of the university is (so) closely tied to the vital interests of the state that state direction was imperative."[84] Having directed his efforts at remodeling the German state system of higher education, Humboldt could not visualize so intricate an organization working without central direction.

Moreover, Humboldt reasoned that state involvement need not be detrimental if certain precepts were respected. First, "knowledge is to be regarded as something not wholly found and never wholly findable, but as something to be searched out."[85] And, second, the state "must hold fast to the inner conviction that if the higher institutions reach their ultimate aim, its own aim, too, will be thereby fulfilled, and from a much loftier point of view than any that could have been arranged directly by the state itself."[86] Humboldt was convinced that a wise government could promote university education with teachers and researchers free to pursue advances in all areas of knowledge. No government could overlook the fact that the "quality of universities was closely related to the immediate public interest of the government."[87] Both long run and short run national development was affected by the quality of the university system.

NOTES

1. E. G. West, *Adam Smith* (New Rochelle, N. Y., 1969), p. 35.

2. Between 1821 and 1837, the greatest educational growth in France was in the availability of schooling, while between 1837 and 1867, schools spread to sparcely populated areas. In the later decades of the nineteenth century, advances were primarily in educational quality. See: Raymond Grew and Patrick Harrigan, with James Whitney, "The Availability of Schooling in Nineteenth Century France," *Journal of Interdisciplinary History*, Vol. 14 (1), p. 561.

3. Mary Joe Maynes, "The Virtues of Archaism: The Political Economy of Schooling in Europe, 1750-1850," *Contemporary Studies in Society and History*, Vol. 21 (4), p. 614.

4. See: Peter V. Meyers, "Professionalization and Societal Change: Rural Teachers in Nineteenth Century France," *Journal of Social History*, Vol. 9 (4), pp. 542-558.

5. Ibid., p. 550.

6. Ibid., p. 552.

7. Maynes, p. 619.

8. Ibid., p. 620.

9. Carla Thomas "Philosophical Anthropology and Educational Change: Wilhelm von Humboldt and the Prussian Reforms," *History of Educational Quarterly*, Vol. 13 (3), p. 220.

10. See: Eric Hopkins, "A Charity School in the Nineteenth Century: Old Swinford Hospital School, 1815-1914," *British Journal of Educational Studies*, Vol. 17 (1), pp. 177-192.

11. Adam Smith, *An Inquiry into the Nature and Causes of the Wealth of Nations*, ed. Edwin Cannan (New York, 1937), p. 717.

12. Ibid.

13. Ibid., p. 265.

14. Ibid., p. 266.

15. John M. Robson, *The Improvement of Mankind* (London, 1968), p. 211.

16. Quoted in E. G. West, "Private versus Public Education, A Classical Economic Dispute" in *The Classical Economists and Economic Policy*, ed. A. W. Coats (London, 1971), p. 136.

17. Herbert Spencer, *The Study of Sociology* (Ann Arbor, 1961), p. 61.

18. Smith, *Wealth of Nations*, p. 717.

19. Ibid.

20. Quoted in West, "Private versus Public Education," p. 126.

21. Ibid.

22. Ibid.

23. Smith, *Wealth of Nations*, p. 719.

24. Ibid., p. 734.

25. James Mill, *On Education*, ed. W. H. Burston (Cambridge, 1969), p. 158; Mill did not want these schools to be affiliated with any religious sect. He thought that if you add a creed "you render necessary a school for each particular creed. ... For this it is in vain to hope that voluntary funds can be provided." Ibid.

26. Jeremy Bentham, "Chrestomathia," *The Works of Jeremy Bentham*, ed. John Bowring (New York, 1962), p. 23.

27. Ibid; see pp. 28-40 for a comprehensive list of the proposed subjects.

28. See: Brian Taylor, "Jeremy Bentham and Church of England Education," *Journal of Educational Studies*, Vol. 27 (2), pp. 154-157.

29. Jeremy Bentham, "Outline of a Work entitled Pauper Management, Improved," *The Works of Jeremy Bentham*, ed. John Bowring (New York, 1962), p. 369.

30. Quoted in West, "Private versus Public Education," p. 131.

31. David Ricardo, *The Works and Correspondence of David Ricardo*, ed. Piero Sraffa (Cambridge, 1952), Vol. VII, pp. 359-360.

32. Ibid.

33. Herbert Spencer, *The Principles of Sociology* (New York, 1923), p. 773.

34. Herbert Spencer, *Facts and Comments* (New York, 1902), p. 82.

35. Ibid.

36. Herbert Spencer, *Social Statics* (New York, 1954), p. 297.

37. Spencer, *The Study of Sociology*, p. 340.

38. Wilhelm von Humboldt, *The Limits of State Action*, ed. J. W. Burrow (Cambridge, 1969), p. 51.

39. Wilhelm von Humboldt, *Humanist Without Portfolio: An Anthology of the Writings of Wilhelm von Humboldt* (Wayne State University Press, 1963), p. 142.

40. Humboldt, *Limits to State Action*, p. 53.

41. Ibid.

42. Frederick Bastiat, *Selected Essays on Political Economy*, ed. George B. deHuszar (New York, 1964), p. 131.

43. Ibid.

44. Ibid.

45. Ibid.

46. Frederick Bastiat, *Economic Harmonies*, ed. George B. deHuszar (New York, 1964), p. 454.

47. Ibid.

48. Quoted in Samuel Hollander, "The Role of the State in Vocational Training," *Southern Economic Journal*, Vol. 34, p. 522; E. G. West claims that Mill had formed his opinions based on an "amateur piece of sociological investigation." See: "Private versus Public Education," p. 132.

49. Quoted in William L. Miller, "The Economics of Education in English Classical Economics," *Southern Economic Journal*, Vol. 32, p. 304.

50. Nassau W. Senior, *Suggestions on Popular Education* (London, 1861), p. 39.

51. Henry Sidgwick, *Principles of Political Economy* (London, 1883), p. 539.

52. Ibid.

53. Henry Sidgwick, *Practical Ethics* (London, 1909), p. 207.

54. Ibid., p. 211.

55. Ibid.

56. Sidgwick, *Principles*, p. 412.

57. Ibid.

58. Ibid.

59. Ibid., p. 419.

60. W. H. G. Armytage, *Four Hundred Years of English Education* (Cambridge, 1970), p. 76; this is the same Mrs. Trimmer who feared the brand of Christianity that Lancaster was serving in his monitorial schools; consequently she encouraged Dr. Bell to compete with Lancaster; Ibid., p. 90.

61. See: Joseph Spengler, "Adam Smith on Human Capital," *The American Economic Review*, Vol. 67 (1), p. 35.

62. Adam Smith, *Lectures on Justice, Police, Revenue and Arms*, ed. Edwin Cannan (Oxford, 1896), p. 236.

63. Miller, p. 300.

64. James Mill, *James Mill and John Stuart Mill on Education*, ed. F. A. Cavanaugh (Cambridge, 1931), p. 66.

65. Ibid.

66. Karl Marx and Friedrich Engles, *Collected Works*, Vol. IV, p. 527.

67. Ibid.

68. Ibid.

69. Marx and Engles, *Collected Works*, Vol. VI, p. 427.

70. Additionally, Marx and Engles held that the true aim of education, total mental enrichment, was unrecognized in bourgeois business training: "The ledger, the desk, business, that is education sufficient, ... but the real education of the mind and storing it with knowledge is not even dreamed of;" *Collected Works*, Vol. VIII, pp. 663-664.

71. David Ward, "The Public Schools and Industry in Britain after 1870, "*The Journal of Contemporary History*, Vol. 2 (3), p. 51.

72. Quoted in West, *Adam Smith*, p. 41.

73. Ibid., p. 42.

74. Smith, *Wealth of Nations*, p. 728.

75. M. L. Clarke, *Classical Education in Britain 1500-1900* (Cambridge, 1959), p. 72.

76. Quoted in Miller, p. 307.

77. For example, in the faculty of law, less than two percent of the students bothered to attend lectures, and exams were more a financial matter than an academic one. See: Theodore Zelden, "Higher Education in France, 1848-1940," in *The Journal of Contemporary History*, Vol. 2 (3), p. 53.

78. Bastiat, *Selected Essays*, p. 240.

79. Ibid.

80. Ibid., p. 241.

81. Ibid., p. 243.

82. Ringer writes that a professor of good quality could earn
     quite a substantial income from his teaching. See: Fritz K.
     Ringer, "Higher Education in Germany in the Nineteenth
     Century," in *The Journal of Contemporary History*, Vol. 2
     (3), pp. 123-138.

83. Daniel Fallon, *The German University: A Heroic Ideal in
     Conflict with the Modern World* (Boulder, Colorado, 1980),
     p. 19.

84. Ibid., p. 25; Humboldt was overwhelmed by the personality
     of the university professor. He wrote to his wife that "to
     direct a group of scholars is not too much better than to
     have a group of comedians under you;" Ibid.

85. Humboldt, *Humanist Without Portfolio*, p. 134.

86. Ibid., p. 136; see also Friedrick Paulsen, *German Education:
     Past and Present* (London, 1908), p. 186.

87. Ibid., p. 140.

CHAPTER VI

THE POLITICAL ECONOMISTS' EDUCATIONAL PLANS

In contriving his ideal plan for educational provision, Adam Smith gathered together all of his notions about the supply of and demand for education. He particularly favored the system followed by the Grecian schools where government noninterference was a predominant feature. In the schools in early Greece, Smith noted that the free market was the main support of the educational services supplied. Government provision was limited to specific types of physical capital, such as places for exercise or performances. The responsibility for education was placed squarely on the shoulders of the parents or guardians of each individual. Additionally, Smith recalled that under the Grecian plan, the state "never assumed any inspection or direction" of parents or guardians.[1] In keeping with the principle of payment in relation to effort, the teachers were paid by fees from the students. Moreover, there were no privileges attendant upon graduation, since presence at school was not necessary in order to practice a particular trade or profession.

Smith discovered that in this unrestricted market, there was no shortage of teachers. Pulled into service by the promise of free market prices, good teachers came forth to teach the most relevant subjects. Smith recorded that "Masters had been found ... for instruction ... in every art and science in which the circumstances of their society rendered it necessary or convenient for them to be instructed. The demand for such instruction produced, what it always produces, the talent for giving it ... ."[2] Smith praised the resourcefulness and initiative of the Grecian instructors and stressed that such talent was motivated only by free market rewards. In the England of his day, Smith observed that the biggest difficulty for people of "rank and fortune" who could easily finance their own education, was finding good teachers. This problem could be alleviated, Smith suggested, by simply following the Grecian example.

However much Smith admired the Greek's plan of education, he was clearly aware that there were many who could not defray their own educational expenses. Smith was firmly convinced that education for the laboring classes was essential to reverse the stultifying effects of the specialization of labor. He sympathized with the overspecialized, uneducated worker who had been rendered "incapable of exerting his strength with vigor and perseverance in any other employment than that to which he has been bred."[3]

The plan Smith chose for educating the poor was similar to

the one used in Scotland. The state would establish a little school in every district "where children may be taught for a reward so moderate, that even a common labourer could afford it."[4] The teacher must be partly paid from the public purse and partly by fees "because if he was wholly, or even principally paid by (the state) he would soon learn to neglect his business."[5] Other necessary elements of a good basic education, according to Smith, included good quality textbooks and a practical curriculum through which the students could learn useful subjects. To give encouragement to the children, small premiums and little badges of distinction would be awarded. Smith did not think the opportunity cost of elementary instruction would be large since he calculated that the basics of reading, writing, and "accounting" could be acquired at an early age before these young people began their "low" occupations.

However Smith realized that even with public provision and social encouragement some children still might not attend school. Because he believed in the microeconomic and macroeconomic importance of universal basic education, Smith decided that the "public ... can even impose upon the whole body of the people the necessity of acquiring those essential parts of education."[6] He presumed that this imposition should take the form of a knowledge requirement rather than compulsory school attendance. His plan included examinations or prohibitions for every man "before he can obtain the freedom in any corporation, or be allowed to set up trade either in a village or town corporate."[7] Smith hoped that by making learning of the essentials of reading and writing necessary to the practice of certain trades, laboring class parents would be more willing to allow their children to attend school.

Some of Smith's ideas on spreading elementary instruction throughout the population were reflected in the thought of J. S. Mill who also supported the concept of public examinations. Mill, too, sought a knowledge requirement rather than compulsory school attendance. Mill considered that there should be a yearly examination "with a gradually extending range of subjects, so as to make the universal acquisition and what is more, retention, of a certain minimum of general knowledge virtually compulsory."[8] Mill's scheme would not only assure basic universal education, but would also go beyond it to monitor the social level of learning and current awareness. As the examination was extended to include more subjects, it could be used as a screening device to ascertain the quantity and quality of knowledge an individual possessed. In fact, Mill crowned his plan with the notion that "all who came up to a certain standard of proficiency might claim a certificate."[9]

Finally, Smith was alert to the problem which attended

religious instruction in schools. The earliest schools were established for the very purpose of imparting religious training, but as the demand for universal education grew, the ability of sectarian schools to supply it in full began to decline. Smith conceded the macroeconomic value of imparting moral teaching to the masses and reasoned that there would be no "injustice" against the people if the cost of this instruction "be defrayed by the general contribution of the whole society."[10] He understood the practical problems involved with trying to implement his plan in a society filled with a variety of religious opinions. So he concluded that it would be preferable at present if the expenses of specific religious training were "defrayed altogether by those who receive the immediate benefit of such education and institution or by the voluntary contribution of those who think they have occasion for either one or the other."[11]

Religion played an indirect part in bringing about an efficient educational system which T. R. Malthus prized. This system, used in Norway, contained a unique blend of social, private, and church supported educational provision. Malthus commented that "there were two free schools ... for the children of the higher classes." In areas like the country parishes where no regular school could be held, "it is the custom for itinerant schoolmasters to go about, and reside for 2 or 3 months in different hamlets." These roving instructors were "supported by the farmers in the neighborhood." The Norway system was so successful, Malthus recorded, that "almost all the common people are able to read, the most of them to write."[12] Once again Malthus pointed out that the knowledge of basic skills produced a peaceful population: "The farmers read the gazettes and talk on political subjects. They are at present contented, which was not quite the case at the commencement of the French Revolution."[13]

According to Malthus the supply of education in this particular system was most adequate, and the demand was quite robust. This strong demand, Malthus explained, was due to the result of a church rule which required a keen knowledge of Luther's catechism for Confirmation. Furthermore, the rite of Confirmation was recognized as a preliminary step to employment, marriage, and the right of inheritance. Therefore, the young person was compelled to master the rudiments of an education before he could be granted the status of an adult. In essence, the Norway system incorporated Smith's suggested "test" for basic literacy through a church regulation.

Jeremy Bentham's educational plans, Chrestomathia and the National Charity Company, definitely did not include any kind of religious instruction. He estimated that to customize universal education to please each religious sect would be to raise its cost prohibitively. Likewise, cost consciousness was the reason

Bentham claimed for promoting the monitorial system of Bell and Lancaster.[14] The scholar teacher principle advocated by Lancaster's educational scheme centered around a scholar who learned as he taught (and, therefore, received little pay); one master was hired to direct and supervise the scholar teachers. Bentham fixed maximum enrollment in each school at 1000 pupils, which, he held, was "generally regarded as the greatest number that in one and the same schoolroom can be taught under constant inspection of one and the same master."[15]

To enable the master teacher to "keep an eye" on all of his charges at once, the schoolhouse was designed following a specific architectural model. The model, similar to Bentham's prison model, Panopticon, was a circular building where the tiers of rooms opened onto a central courtyard. This specific design would also be cost saving since there would be "one general superintendent; one apparatus for warming; the same for lighting; (and) one set of implements employed as instruments of instruction."[16] Bentham's knack for ferreting out economies of mass production obviously excelled in his plans for school construction.[17]

As unusual as Bentham's school building style might be, his proposed Chrestomathic method was very practical and progressive for its time. He emphasized pedagogical principles which were subsequently to become standard educational practice. Among these were "place-capturing" where emulation and competition replaced corporal punishment to stimulate intellectual advance, visual aids of art and wall diagrams to maximize and to reinforce learning, and grouping children according to their ability to expedite collective instruction. Each facet of the child's environment was directed toward maximizing learning while minimizing cost.

The funding of Chrestomathia was by subscription, so money raising for its development was begun. At first Bentham had offered his own garden as a site for the intended school but later changed his mind. This was an indication that the ever erratic Bentham was ready to focus his energies on other projects. In 1814, James Mill, an ardent supporter of the enterprise, wrote to Francis Place that Bentham was losing his enthusiasm for Chrestomathia. Mill cited Bentham's making "so many difficulties" regarding the choice of a place for the school.[18] Moreover, community objections to the school were growing. David Ricardo, a representative of the site selection committee, had put a bid on a property on Leicester Square; he was forced to withdraw the offer because of the agitation of area property owners who mistrusted an avowed nonreligious school. By 1822, Chrestomathia was an abandoned project and subscriber funds were returned.

Bentham had even less luck with his National Charity Company proposal which was devised for the education of the poor. Indigent children would both work and receive an education in "Industry Houses."[19] Bentham elaborated on the physical construction of these buildings and detailed the mechanics for making the scheme operate. The children would study intensely when very young and then be placed in apprentice programs, at which time their education would continue on Sundays and whenever else practical. These apprentices and their pauper masters would produce their goods on the premises of the National Charity Company, which was the sole agent for the sale of the products. This pauper labor would be used to turn a profit for the owners of the company which was "instituted on mercantile principles" like the East India Company.[20] In addition to the original capital to be subscribed by private investors, the institution would receive an annual subsidy from the government equal to the poor rates. Capitalized like a joint stock company, guaranteed a handsome subsidy from the government each year, and employing extremely low cost labor, the National Charity Company could not fail to earn an attractive return for its owners, Bentham deduced.

Furthermore, the National Charity Company plan would replace outdoor relief to the benefit of the poor, Bentham forcefully maintained. Pauper children would be housed and fed and educated in a healthy environment where they would learn a productive skill, and not be exposed to the dangers of the sordid workhouses. In addition fiscal justice would be served since the "contribution" for the support of this system would be on "willing" investors, not on unwilling taxpayers.[21] Tax rates would not rise; investor capital would be used in its stead. Bentham had no doubt that a privately owned company would be more cost efficient than a program run by the government and wrote that the National Charity Company would be "of *thrifty* management in every respect greater."[22]

To encourage investor interest in his plan Bentham specified the returns to be anticipated from the National Charity Company schools in his "prospectus":

> The proper end of education is no other than the proper end of life - wellbeing. The wellbeing here in question is, partly that of the individual to be educated, partly that of the parties at whose expense, and by whose care, he is to be educated - viz. the proposed company: ... in respect of the wellbeing of the child, they are as guardians; in respect of their own, they are as masters.[23]

Bentham advertised that both those educated and those investing capital would receive ample advantages from this proposed educational scheme.

Bentham had such hopes for the success of the National Charity Company that he envisioned the parents of the "superior classes" voluntarily enrolling their children as apprentices in the Industry Houses. However, his enthusiasm was not well founded, as the project progressed only as far as a circulated appeal for funding for research and promotion.[24] Nothing more seems to have been done to bring the National Charity Company to life.

Bastiat and Spencer were avid apologists for an educational system which relied on simplicity rather than on the construction of a complex learning scheme. They both praised the free market in their suggested educational plans. Bastiat, writing under the heavy hand of state monopolized education, challenged the national legislature to allow three sources of education, the state, the clergy, and free teachers, to exist side by side. He emphasized that the latter should be truly free "to try new and fruitful methods in their instruction."[25] He persisted, "Let the state university teach what it cherishes, Greek and Latin; let the clergy teach what it knows, Greek and Latin. Let both of them produce Platonists and demagogues; but let them not prevent us from training, by other methods, men for our country and for our century."[26] Bastiat credited the free market with the ability to furnish all of the educational services that a nation needed to grow and prosper. He petitioned the government to permit the free schools "to try at their own peril and risk, a Christian and scientific curriculum. The experiment is worth making. Who knows? Perhaps it would be an advance."[27] Bastiat relied upon an unfettered market system to produce a solution to the problem of relevant education. He queried, "Can it be doubted that education ... would venture under the stimulus of competition, into new and fruitful paths?"[28] Competitive education would be "genuine education," education which could truly benefit society, and would prevail when the schools were freed from government control, Bastiat imagined.

Spencer, who decried the "rage for uniformity" which had begun to permeate society in all aspects, including education, recalled a story about the French educational experience, a story that surely would have interested Bastiat. Spencer related the account of the French "minister who boasted that at a given hour all the boys in France were saying the same lesson."[29] This, Spencer said, was "the outcome of a nature which values equality more than liberty."[30] The equality provided by the French educational system resulted in mediocrity, he thought. Spencer, as Bastiat, rated competition in a free market educational scheme highly; he issued this warning: "competition in methods of education is all-essential and anything that tends to diminish competition will be detrimental."[31] Furthermore, Spencer thought that growing state involvement in education put private schools "more and more to disadvantage." And, consequently, as state schools replace private institutions "there results an increase in uniformity."[32] He recognized that "by each fresh Act of Parliament" educational organizations were becoming more rigid, less competitive.[33]

Spencer wrote "the law of suply and demand extends from the material sphere to the mental sphere, and that as interference with the supply and demand of commodities is mischievous, so is interference with the supply and demand of a cultured faculty."[34] Consumer satisfaction was the best guide to what was taught, as well as to what was bought, Spencer insisted, since "in the long run, the interest of the consumer is not only an efficient guarantee for the goodness of the things consumed, but the best guarantee."[35] Education must be bought and sold in the marketplace where "price is a tolerable safe index of value," Spencer concluded.[36] He certainly would have applauded the Scottish schools of Smith's day which had made good use of the pricing mechanism to sell instruction in many individual subjects.

Spencer's writings were woefully out of date since the question of an educational system free of government was marginally debatable in Britain after the Factory Act of 1833 was passed. This legislation stipulated that workers between the ages of nine and thirteen attend school for two hours a day, six days a week. Factory inspectors were hired to verify compliance with this act. The law required that the child present a voucher to his employer on Monday stating that he or she had been to school during the previous week. If there were no schools available in the area, the factory was responsible for furnishing a place for learning. The employers objected strongly to having to finance these ad hoc schools. The government responded to the factory owners' appeals by issuing maintenance grants to existing schools to enable them to increase their operating facilities.[37] It was curious that the British government became involved in education to relieve the financial distress of perhaps the strongest proponents of free market education, the upper income industrialists.

J. R. McCulloch chose to focus his attention on the grant system which Parliament implemented to aid in the spread and maintenance of schools accessible to working children. He judged it "one of the best (educational schemes) that can be devised."[38] McCulloch pointed out that under Parliament's maintenance grants, the state did not establish schools, but confined itself to giving assistance to most types of existing schools under certain conditions. Free market elements could be retained under this system where variety would remain in the classroom to the extent that it was useful and the responsibility for appointing qualified school-masters would rest with the individual educational institution. The question of "appropriate" religious instruction would not be raised, McCulloch argued, as the religious instruction prevalent in the school would remain as long as it fulfilled the needs of the students and their parents.

The state manifested its presence through the granting or withholding of financial aid to the school and through public censure following inspection of the institution. McCulloch explained that under Parliament's grant system, since the state examined the schools that it assisted financially it could ascertain which schools complied with established state standards. The results of the state inspection would routinely be publicized in each school district; forcing the schools to provide quality instruction or face public criticism. McCulloch hoped that this plan would cause teachers and administrators to be attentive to their duties since the system would reward those who performed well and identify those who did not.

Unlike some of the other classical economists, Nassau Senior was optimistic about the financial future of education. He esti-mated that educational expenses could successfully be met par-tially through the use of private sector funding. He envisioned a scheme of voluntary contributions to education existing side by side with taxes collected for this purpose. In fact Senior would recommend that taxes be collected for education *only* "in cases in which voluntary contributions do not exist or are trifling."[39] Senior concurred with McCulloch as to the benefits of the grant system of Parliament, but desired to include a special provision in the education legislation to protect the privately financed insti-tution. He urged, "If a rate-supported school were established in a parish already possessing a voluntarily supported school, contributions to the latter school should be allowed in respect to the rate."[40] Under Senior's scheme parents who paid tuition to a nonpublic school would deduct this payment from their school taxes. This plan would allow parents to choose the services of a rate-supported school or of a privately supported school, paying only for whichever type they selected. In this way, the private institutions would not be doubly disadvantaged in their attempt to compete with state maintained education.

Senior's opinion of social gains from universal education, furnished either by the state or by private sources, remained lofty. He recognized that through widespread education "we ... (would give) to the present generation an education which will fit them to educate still better another generation, which in time, may further improve a third."[41] The culmination of this compre-hensive schooling would be, according to Senior, "an Utopia inhabited by a self-educated and well-educated labouring population."[42]   Senior knew that this could be a reality if the state would pass laws to encourage schools supported both by taxes and by private funds.

Senior's bid for financial justice for parents who chose to pay for private schooling was not new in his day and was a topic of political consideration for centuries after its inception.[43]   For example, Tom Paine, of the late 1700s, was affected by the rising tax burden on British families.   He discovered that increases in the poor rates had *caused* families to neglect their children's education because the reduction in their disposable income left them unable to afford the tuition in a private or a church sponsored school.   Therefore, if parents desired to avoid state supported schools for religious or other reasons, their children went untaught.   To avoid this outcome, Paine suggested that each pupil be supplied by the state with an education allowance of 10 shillings a year " ... for the expense of schooling for six years each, and half-a-crown a year for paper and spelling books."[44]   The children (through their parents) would be permitted to spend their school allowance in whatever school they found most desirable.   This "voucher" scheme would promote a healthy competition among schools since consumer choice would determine the success and profitability of an educational institution.

About one hundred years after Tom Paine, a French parliamentary commission examining educational finance, advocated parental free choice in school selection through the use of educational allowances or the "bon scolaire."   The commission reported that "the community pays the school fees on (the parents') behalf, but to one particular teacher; the father of a needy family thus finds himself deprived of the freedom to choose between the various schools in which he has confidence, and sometimes is compelled either to entrust his child to a teacher in whom he has no confidence or to let the child grow up in ignorance."[45]   The commission advised: "Instead of granting the children who are entitled to free education the right of admission to one particular school, give them a "bon scolaire," a draft payable to bearer by the local treasury on presentation and valid for all schools in the community."[46]   The implementation of such a scheme would be advantageous to all, the commission concluded: "The poor will thus have regained their freedom, charity will have lost its bitter taste, and our laws will once again have averred the respect which is due to the liberty of human conscious."[47]   Unfortunately, the commission's recommendation did not have enough support among the French legislators and was quietly shelved in 1873.

John Stuart Mill presented educational suggestions similar to those of Senior and McCulloch; however, he did not go so far as

101

to actually propose educational allowances or tax reductions. He penned: "If the Government would make up its mind to require for every child a good education, it might save itself the trouble of providing one. It might leave to parents to obtain the education where and how they pleased, and content itself with helping to pay the school fees of the poorer classes of children, and defraying the entire school expenses of those who have no one else to pay for them."[48] In specifying the particulars of state requirements for education, much of what Mill recommended was explained by McCulloch when he examined the grant system. Mill held strongly to the conviction that "all parents should be required to have their children taught certain things, being left free to select the teachers, but the efficiency of teaching being insured by a Government inspection of schools ... ."[49] Optimistic about the financial arrangements of such a school system, Mill continued, "the actual provision of schools by a local rate would not necessarily be required if any schools already existing in the locality were sufficient for the purpose, or which could be made so by aid from local funds and inspection."[50]

A government administrative department would be required, Mill said, to regulate the public funds which would flow into the school system. But this department would not be permitted control over the teachers or over subject matter. Mill felt that the existence of a department to administer school funds must not mean that "the teachers ... be appointed or directly controlled by any public office." Selection of teachers would rest best in a school committee chosen from the locality, he decided.

In Mill's view of education, private schools would necessarily exist side by side with state institutions; as he said, "It is one thing to provide schools and colleges, and another to require that no person shall act as an instructor of youth without a government license."[51] State established education must be but "one among many competing experiments, carried on for the purpose of example and stimulus to keep the others up to a certain standard of excellence."[52] Unlike J. B. Say who feared that government provided education would prove to be the superior competitor, forcing private education out of business, Mill considered that "if the country contains a sufficient number of persons qualified to provide education under government auspices, the same persons would be able and willing to give an equally good education on the voluntary principle."[53] Mill must have visualized some type of grant-voucher scheme where consumers were free to choose either privately or publicly funded education and where quality of instruction would be rewarded through free market prices. He certainly recognized the financial superiority of a state supported school and he went on record opposing the efficacy of voluntary contributions to furnish basic education. Only through a hybrid state-private financial arrangement could private schools remain competitive in the market.

Mill's educational plan had a final important similarity to the early classicals, an examination of the pupil's competency. Recall that Mill had called for "a real and searching examination" of pupils "through a test to be administered by the state which would serve as a check on the quality of education which was being provided."[54] Furthermore, Mill proposed "to prevent the State from exercising through these (testing) arrangements, an improper influence over opinion, the knowledge required for passing an examination should ... be confined to facts and positive science exclusively."[55] Mill's specification of factual queries was another indication of his awareness of the need to guard individual thought and beliefs in an area touched by government control.

In the *Communist Manifesto*, Karl Marx and Friedrich Engles detailed their educational plan which was contingent upon government control. The *Manifesto* contained the specific elements of the educational system of the new order. There were three fundamental changes in the "old" education which Marx and Engles advocated: (1) "Free education for all children in public schools; (2) abolition of childrens' factory labour in its present form; and (3) combination of education with industrial production."[56] First, their quest centered on the search for true universal education; they were not satisfied with the minimal compliance with factory education legislation that they had witnessed in some countries. They favored complete education for all children in schools supported by the state. Second, Marx and Engles were appalled by the physical and mental abuse which afflicted children factory workers. To them the plight of children in the factories was one of the most serious social evils spawned by the capitalistic system. They demanded that the practice of sending small children into the work place to be treated as senseless pieces of machinery cease. Finally, in the *Manifesto*, Marx and Engles referred to an experimental educational method, "education combined with production," which they would particularize at a later date.

In *Capital* Marx introduced his plan for the practical education of society. He started, oddly enough, by praising the Factory Acts for proclaiming "elementary education to be an indispensable condition to the employment of children."[57] These acts had initiated a novel type of training he continued, one in which "manual labour (was combined) with education and gymnastics."[58] Marx referred to the recent observations of Nassau Senior and to the reports from the factory inspectors which attested to the *harm* caused by schooling devoid of work. They concluded that this method of instruction wasted "the time, health, and energy of the children." [59]

103

Then Marx commended the workers' technical schools, "ecoles d'enseignement professionel," as path-breaking attempts to instruct the children of the workers in the technological and practical aspects of working with machinery.[60] He applauded the success of this type of school in a capitalist society as evidence of "one step already spontaneously taken towards effecting revolution."[61] Marx eagerly awaited the growth of technological education in the new social order: "There can be no doubt that when the working class comes into power, as inevitably it must, technical instruction both theoretical and practical, will take its proper place in the working class schools."[62]

To Marx, the provision of technical training for the workers was another strike in "the abolition of the old division of labour." Instruction for the workers in the mechanics of production was diametrically opposed to the continuance of a capitalistic system which depended on mindless labor with no control over its environment or circumstance. When educated technicians could understand and even change industrial processes, Marx expected the dividing lines between labor and capital to be obliterated.

Lastly, in *Anti-Duhring*, Engles solidified the Marxian position on education. In this work, Engles stressed once again the necessity of "practical training in an educational scheme which combined work and instruction."[63] Engles acclaimed Marx's critique of the Factory Acts and judged that in Marx's works the description of the socialistic school of the future was complete. Engles repeated Marx's blast against powerless education begrudgingly given to the masses by the bourgeoisie. To Engles, as to Marx, the only type of meaningful education was practical education - education that would furnish the worker with the tools to subjugate his capitalist boss.

In a manner similar to Marx, Henry Fawcett recognized the wastes of misapplied education. He wondered at the wisdom of political and social decision makers who denied education to the poor gifted child and squandered it on the dull rich student. He suggested that the costly social misuse of precious educational resources could be relieved somewhat even within a privately funded school system by giving the children of the poor equal opportunity to compete with the children of the rich for scholarships and fellowships. More importantly, Fawcett concurred with Marx's observations that current school techniques led to a dull and routine school experience. He, too, praised the Factory Acts and noted that the fifteen hour school requirements for employed children could be a very effective means to a good education. The main attribute of this system, Fawcett wrote, was that "the alternate working and schooling mutually assist one another; school is a relief from work, and work is a relief from school."[64]

104

The proposals of the classical political writers on educational systems ran the gamut from free market profit maximizing schemes to plans of total government provision and control. Many writers suggested alternatives in between the two extremes, searching for ways to finance the education of large numbers of impoverished children, while adhering to the classical principles of justice and liberty. This was not an easy task even at the outset, but their feelings of futility were compounded by the fact that as the ink dried on their recommendations, new legislation was being enacted which would preclude the consideration of their ideas for decades or even for centuries.

COST AND CURRICULUM

The classical economists' grand educational plans were definitely diverse. In some cases it would be difficult to find any common ground between them. However, there were concerns in the educational plans of almost all the writers which did coincide; these were the considerations of cost and curriculum. The political economists were naturally inspired to discuss cost, since the heart of their science deals with the search for cost efficiency. Additionally, they were led by a desire to be both modern and thorough when they ventured upon observations of what should be included in the school curriculum. Their ideas on cost, and to some extent on school curriculum, were based in part on religious considerations.

As an economist, one fact was clear to James Mill: "Is abundantly evident, that what is to be done for the poor voluntarily and extensively, most be done cheaply. It is equally evident, that in most cases, what is to be done most cheaply ought to be done on the largest possible scale."[65] Mill continued with the idea that to reap economies of large scale production, a uniform curriculum was necessary, one which precluded specific religious instruction. Remember that Mill had written that if you "teach the children only reading and writing, ... you may teach the whole children of a populous city in one school. Add to this a religious creed, and you must then have many schools; one for every denomination of Christian ... ." So he completed this thought, "let the teacher of reading and writing be he who can do it best; and let him keep his religion entirely to himself."[66]

Nassau Senior likewise would favor the restriction of religious instruction in the public schools. He spoke of the financial burden imposed on the state when it was forced to supply schools with separate religious instruction, as in the case of Ireland. Senior found these arrangements not only to be costly, but also to yield lower quality education. He deduced that this inefficiency resulted "from the frequent necessity of having in the same district three or four small schools, with inferior arrangements and inferior masters, instead of one good one."[67]   Furthermore, Senior, who had spent many hours inspecting the schools, pointed out that the practice of having schools of various religious denominations led to hostility among the students.   Rather than fostering a spirit of community and goodwill, the separation of schools into different religious sects was creating rival factions among the young.

Fawcett was somewhat upset by the public desire to build schools of many denominations, but he was particularly disturbed by the public squandering of those denominational schools already constructed.   He viewed the bias against using church supported or privately supported schools for public education both a social waste and a private extravagance which would have seriously detrimental long-range effects to society as a whole. Fawcett judged that "when there is a denominational school within a stone's throw of the child's home, is it not perfectly monstrous that an ill-clad child should be compelled in all weathers, in snow and in rain, to walk two or three miles to a Board school, in order that effect may be given to the conscientious scruples of sensitive ratepayers."[68]   Moreover, Fawcett foresaw that society itself stood to be the loser in the long run from the demise of private schools, as public schools gradually replaced them.   The increase in schools established and maintained by the state would mean an increase in taxes and an increase in taxpayers' complaints.   Along with the determination of the kinds of schools which should exist, the state also specified the amount of time students must legally spend in school.   Fawcett was alarmed by the restrictions on liberty which state supported compulsory education produced.   He felt that citizens who considered themselves free must strongly object to any type of compulsion for its own sake.   But add to this the ignominious requirements of having to send their children to "objectionable" schools, and Fawcett imagined, the parents might rebel.

Religious considerations certainly affected cost concepts in the educational ideas of the political economists, but religion also played a key role in the early classical ideas on curriculum. Smith, Bentham, and James Mill all thought that religion was under the purview of domestic education and, therefore, religious education should remain in the home.   However, a contrary practice commonly prevailed in the schools established by religious groups and in endowed schools which followed the wishes of their founders.   Often these requests included instruction in a specific religion, as well as instruction in specific subjects. [69]   Even though much basic religious education was furnished in the home, middle and upper class school children were usually subjected to religious doctrine along with the rudiments of reading and writing.

Adam Smith searched for balance in the subject matter in elementary schools. He desired that these schools furnish "the necessary introduction to the most sublime as well as the most useful sciences." [70] His plan included the practical idea of making childrens' readers more "instructive" (not by including lessons on British law, as Bentham had envisioned) and reducing the time spent on teaching students "a smattering of Latin ... which can scarce ever be of any use to them." [71] Among the subjects that should be included in the curriculum Smith insisted that "the elementary parts of geometry and mechanics "would keep the common people in good stead since "there is scarce a common trade which does not afford some opportunities of apply-ing to it the principles of geometry and mechanics ... ." [72]

John Baptiste Say, as Smith, considered that the practi-tioners of skilled trades could benefit through practical types of universal education, especially in the fields of "Agriculture, Arts, and Commerce." Furthermore, unlike Smith, Say included moral education as part of citizenship training. Finally, Say's plea for basic education in the three R's was based on the idea of enabling men to develop their potential productivity to the fullest by giving them a firm foundation upon which to build the special knowledge required for their occupations.

T. R. Malthus refuted the opinions of Smith and Say re-garding the usefulness of geometry and mechanics to the common laborer. Malthus considered these subjects too complex to be taught to the worker. Nevertheless, Malthus decided that the ramifications of population pressures were simple enough to be explained sufficiently to the poor. Moreover, instruction could easily be provided to the laborer on how to ameliorate the popu-lation situation. Furthermore, Malthus held the difficulty of comprehending economics somewhere between geometry and me-chanics and population pressures. He was firmly convinced of the need for instruction in political economy and he wrote: if "a few of the simplest principles of Political Economy could be added to the instructions ..., the benefit to Society would be almost incalcuable." [73]

McCulloch's idealized school curriculum was broad. The main elements in a "useful" system of public education were reading and writing, McCulloch agreed. Additionally, he promoted the Malthusian idea that a good education should include instruction in the seriousness of parental responsibility and suggestions on the possibility of choosing late marriages to prepare properly for parental duties. In contrast to other classical writers, McCulloch had no objections to instructing students in the duties "enjoined by religion and morality." Instruction in these subjects was included in his analysis of human capital development. He reasoned that workers who were morally responsible would give a full day's work when they punched the clock, and as a consequence, productivity would rise. Moreover, they would increase the national product through their extra work effort, McCulloch decided.

In a similar context, McCulloch deduced that if men were taught that they were responsible for their own fate, they would be able to react favorably to changes in their economic environment. Therefore, he held that the workers should be instructed in the circumstances which elevate or depress the rate of wages. If the worker had control over any of these conditions, he would have some measure of control over his own future. Lastly, in McCulloch's educational curriculum, there would be basic instruction in health and sanitation measures. He strongly endorsed the idea that healthy workers were more productive and, therefore, a useful system of education must include instruction on physical well-being. This notion was also in keeping with McCulloch's theory of human capital accumulation.

James Mill was severly dissatisfied with the educational opportunities available to the upwardly mobile middle class youth of his day. In contrast to a purely traditional curriculum, the education Mill envisioned would be filled with "useful" and "practical" subjects such as mathematics, foreign languages, and political and moral sciences.[74] Mill asked Jeremy Bentham to work out the details for such a school and from this collaboration, Chrestomathia was born. Bentham responded vigorously to Mill's suggested subjects. He set up the Chrestomatic curriculum beginning with technology, arithmetic, physics, and natural sciences and, almost a score of pages later, concluded with the humanities.[75]

The humanities were not on the approved curriculum list for National Charity Company schools. In fact, for his pauper pupils, Bentham desired "exemption from intellectual exercise of the most painful kind," especially the learning of languages.[76] He considered that most of what passed for a "liberal education" was actually painful and useless to these poor students. According to Bentham, the "useful studies" for National Charity Company students included natural history, chemistry, mechanics, mathematics, agriculture, gardening, medicine (for veterinary purposes) and politics and constitutional law.[77] Oddly enough, Bentham sang the praises of music education as a way to foster morality. In a particularly wild moment, he even considered the institution of a "National Music Seminary" to fill up the "vacuum of the mind" and ultimately render productivity increases among the song-filled workers.

John Stuart Mill pressed for the basics in elementary education but was especially concerned with the subjects offered in higher education. In 1867 he put forth a wide range view of education in his "Inaugural Address at the University of St. Andrews": "Whatever helps to shape the human being, to make the individual what he is or to hinder him from what he is not, is part of his education."[78] But Mill also knew that education went beyond the limits of the individual to form "the culture which each generation purposely gives to those who are to be its successors in order to qualify them for at least keeping up, and if possible for raising, the level of improvement which has been attained."[79] To the point, Mill stated clearly that he believed in compromise in higher education. To him the balanced curriculum would contain "the light of general culture" and would "direct the use of professional knowledge" and would also "illuminate the technicalities of a special pursuit."[80] Mill asked directly: "Can anything desire the name of a good education which does not include literature and science, too?"[81]

Mill advocated poetry for elevating the mind. In a speech at the London Debating Society, Mill attempted to recount what he had learned from Wordsworth many years before when he was in dire need of spiritual reinforcement. Mill's experience led him to claim poetry as "an important branch of education. Education is (1) the education of the intellect and (2) that of the feelings. (There is) folly (in) supposing that the first suffices without the last."[82] Since poetry sustains the feelings, it also supports the intellect, Mill averred. In "traditional" classical fashion, Mill wrote that Greek and Roman literature, too, were essential for sharpening intellectual development, although he recorded that teaching living languages was mostly a waste of time because these languages could be learned in "a few months in the country itself." Finally, he lamented that direct moral and religious teaching was really "beyond the sphere" of public education, since these consisted in training the feelings and daily habits. As his father, Mill still preferred religion to remain a subject for early domestic education. However, he acknowledged that a university had an indirect moral influence over its students since they imbibed its culture during their studies there. Although Mill's own education was essentially of the liberal classical variety, he judged that elements of both classical education and scientific education should be incorporated in sound a curriculum of higher learning, with just enough instruction in the arts and poetry to support robust mental health.

Bastiat presented his observations on the content of higher education of his day, especially on the emphasis on classical subjects. The irrelevance of what was taught in the traditional curriculum annoyed Bastiat less than the lessons that *were* learned from the "abuse of classical studies." He contended that "the judgment and morality of the country" had been perverted by this wrong headed instruction. More specifically, Bastiat blasted, "I say that the subversive doctrines called *socialism* or *communism* are the fruits of classical education."[83] His justification for this bold statement lay in his claim that "the soul of France (was) penetrated, along with the language of the Romans, by their ideas, their sentiments, their opinions, and a caricature of their manners and customs."[84] Thus classical education "was a melange of false ideas, brutal sentiments, subversive utopias, and fatal experiments."[85] To Bastiat there was no mystery why the students of France were prone to revolution. He believed that "under the influence of classical education, political life cannot be anything but an interminable series of struggles and revolutions to determine which utopian is to have the prerogative of making experiments on the people as if they were raw material."[86] Bastiat displayed a unique attitude among the classical economists of his day toward traditional subjects in the higher education curriculum. Although most social scientists sought curriculum change, few would go so far as to accuse the cultural tradition of Greek and Latin studies of promoting subversive activities.

NOTES

1. Adam Smith, *An Inquiry into the Nature and Causes of the Wealth of Nations*, ed. Edwin Cannan (New York, 1937), p. 730.

2. Ibid.

3. Ibid., p. 735.

4. Ibid., p. 737.

5. Ibid.

6. Ibid.

7. Ibid., p. 738.

8. Quoted in E. G. West, *Education and the Industrial Revolution* (New York, 1975), p. 161.

9. Ibid.

10. Quoted in Pierre N. V. Tu, "The Classical Economists and Education," *Kyklos*, Vol. 22, p. 694.

11. Ibid.

12. T. R. Malthus, *The Travel Diaries of Thomas Robert Malthus*, ed. Patricia James (Cambridge, 1966), p. 167.

13. Ibid., p. 175.

14. Bentham's most severe attack on the Church of England occurred in 1818 when he accused the church of deriding Lancaster's success. In Lancaster's schools the Bible was used as a teaching aid and Bentham claimed that the church feared that "the Bible might prevail over the Catechism and the Church of England might thus be brought to an end;" quoted in West, *Education and the Industrial Revolution*, p. 129.

15. Quoted in Elissa S. Itzen, "Bentham's 'Chrestomathia': Utilitarian Legacy to English Education," *Journal of the History of Ideas*, Vol. 39 (2), p. 308.

16. Ibid., p. 309.

17. Ibid., p. 304.

18. Ibid., p. 315.

19. See Brian Taylor, "A Note in Response to Itzen's "Bentham's 'Chrestomathia': Utilitarian Legacy to English Education," *Journal of the History of Ideas*, Vol. 43 (2), pp. 309-314.

20. Bentham estimated a 300% profit from male adult labor. See: Gertrude Himmelfarb, "Bentham's Utopia: The National Charity Company," *The Journal of British Studies*, Vol. 10 (1), p. 106.

21. Jeremy Bentham, "Outline of a Work entitled Pauper Management Improved," *The Works of Jeremy Bentham*, ed. John Bowring (New York, 1962), p. 369.

22. Ibid.

23. Ibid.

24. Himmelfarb, p. 123.

25. Frederick Bastiat, *Selected Essays on Political Economy*, ed. George B. deHuszar (New York, 1964), p. 277.

26. Ibid.

27. Ibid., p. 279.

28. Ibid., p. 286.

29. Herbert Spencer, *The Principles of Sociology* (New York, 1923), p. 597.

30. Ibid.

31. Quoted in David Duncan, *Life and Letters of Herbert Spencer* (New York, 1908), Vol. II, p. 127.

32. Ibid., p. 197.

33. Spencer, *The Principles of Sociology*, p. 586.

34. Herbert Spencer, *Facts and Comments* (New York, 1902), p. 83.

35. Herbert Spencer, *Social Statics* (New York, 1954), p. 301.

36. Quoted in David Wiltshire, *The Social and Political Thought of Herbert Spencer* (Oxford, 1978), p. 143.

37. See: W. H. G. Armytage, *Four Hundred Years of English Education* (Cambridge, 1970), p. 111.

38. Quoted in D. P. O'Brien, *J. R. McCulloch* (London, 1970), p. 401.

39. Nassau Senior, *Suggestions on Popular Education* (London, 1862), p. 57.

40. Ibid., p. 59.

41. Ibid, p. 5.

42. Ibid.

43. See: Milton Friedman in Robert Solo's *Economics and the Public Interest* (Rutgers, New Jersey, 1955), and E. G. West, *Nonpublic School Aid* (Lexington, Massachusetts, 1976) and Mark Blaug, *The Economics of Education* (London, 1972), especially pp. 307-317.

44. Quoted in E. G. West, "Tom Paine's Voucher Scheme for Public Education," *Southern Economic Journal*, Vol. 3 (3), p. 381.

45. Quoted in W. Van Vliet and J. G. Smyth, "A Nineteenth Century French Proposal to Use School Vouchers," in *Comparative Education Review*, Vol. 26 (1), p. 99.

46. Ibid.

47. Ibid., p. 99-100.

48. John Stuart Mill, *On Liberty*, ed. Currin V. Shields (New York, 1956), p. 129.

49. John Stuart Mill, *The Letters of John Stuart Mill*, ed. Hugh S. R. Elliot (New York, 1910), Vol, II, pp. 101-102.

50. Ibid., p. 106.

51. John Stuart Mill, *Principles of Political Economy*, ed. William Ashley (Fairfield, 1976), p. 942.

52. Mill, *Liberty*, p. 129.

53. Ibid.

54. Mill, *Letters*, p. 106.

55. Mill, *Liberty*, p. 129.

56. Karl Marx and Friedrich Engles, *Manifesto of the Communist Party* (Moscow, 1977), p. 75.

57. Karl Marx, *Capital* (Moscow, 1948), Vol. I, p. 453.

58. Ibid., pp. 453-454.

59. Ibid.; the Factory inspectors reported superior progress for "Half-timers" who went to school 15 hours and to the factory the rest of the week. They held that these students did as well as, and often better than, the students who attended school for the full 30 hours. See: West, *Education and the Industrial Revolution*, (New York, 1975), pp. 144-145.

60. In France in 1758, the Ecole des arts of Amiens, and in 1779, the Ecole nationales militaries had each begun a curriculum filled with technical subjects including manufacturing, commerce, and agriculture. In Glasglow in 1823, a "mechanics class" leased an unused chapel and started a Mechanics' Institution. See: "Institutional Innovation in Popular Education in Eighteenth Century France: Two Examples" by Harvey Chisick in *French Historial Studies*, Vol. 10 (1), pp. 41-73 and Armytage, pp. 98-99.

61. Marx, *Capital*, p. 458.

62. Ibid.

113

63. Friedrich Engles, *Anti-Duhring* (Moscow, 1975), pp. 377–382.

64. Henry Fawcett, *Pauperism: Its Causes and Remedies* (New York, 1871), p. 129.

65. James Mill, *On Education*, ed. W. H. Burston (Cambridge, 1969), p. 134.

66. Ibid., pp. 131–132.

67. Nassau W. Senior, *Industrial Efficiency and Social Economy*, ed. S. Leon Levy (New York, 1928), p. 343.

68. Henry Fawcett, *Speeches on Some Current Political Questions* (London, 1873), p. 116.

69. Richard S. Thompson argues in "The English Grammar School Curriculum in the 18th Century: A Reappraisal" that the English grammar school curriculum had more flexibility than is commonly believed; see the *British Journal of Educational Studies*, Vol. 19 (1), pp, 32–39.

70. Smith, *Wealth of Nations*, pp. 737–738.

71. Ibid.

72. Ibid.

73. T. R. Malthus, *An Essay on the Principle of Population* (London, 1806), p. 416.

74. Itzen, p. 304.

75. The exact list of Bentham's suggested subjects can be found in "Chrestomathia", pp. 28–40.

76. Himmelfarb, p. 105.

77. Ibid., pp. 106–107. Bentham, as Smith, would have this instruction take place in a concentrated fashion before the child could become actively engaged in an apprenticeship program and, after that time, only on Sundays. Since Bentham believed that age four was right for beginning work, this limited the child's period of instruction to a minimal length of time; Ibid., p. 105.

78. John Stuart Mill, *John Stuart Mill on Education*, ed. Francis W. Garforth (New York, 1971), p. 154.

79. Ibid.

80. Ibid., p. 156.

81. Ibid., p. 160.

82. Quoted in R. J. Halliday, *John Stuart Mill* (New York, 1976), p. 28.

83. Bastiat, *Selected Essays*, p. 245.

84. Ibid., p. 246.

85. Ibid., p. 267.

86. Ibid., p. 274.

CHAPTER VII

CLASSICAL OPINIONS OF THE STATE IN EDUCATION

Many problems confronted the economic educational policy maker in the late eighteenth and early nineteenth centuries. The most obvious one was that the quantity and quality of schools freely supplied under a predominantly voluntary system were considerably less than what was needed to achieve basic universal literacy. [1] Another hinderance to the spread of elementary instruction was the presence of specific religious instruction in the private or endowed schools; this impeded the attendance at these schools of children from religious homes who believed in a different creed. Finally, the large diversity of teacher skill levels led to the cry for some type of teacher certification. Those studying possible kinds of national educational supply were becoming increasingly interested in a uniform system of instruction.

The demand for universal basic education was hampered most by parental indifference which was often rooted in parental ignorance. The political economists had often written how educational attitudes were passed unchanged from generation to generation. To break the chain of negative feelings about the benefits of education, an outside force would have to be employed, some reasoned. Furthermore, the opportunity cost of schooling made it very difficult for poor families to choose education for their children over work. Since the economists included the concept of rationality in describing the people who made up the economy, they sympathized with the predicament of poor parents. They also knew that rational individual parental choice might postpone the dissemination of knowledge to the poor for a long time.

Nevertheless, in general, the political thinkers were hesitant about legislating compulsory school attendance. The effect of a compulsory education law on the individual and society would be overwhelming. It would touch every household and affect every child's life. Therefore, when the first compulsory rules were made, they were in the form of an education requirement for employment rather than for forced education directly. Then, when specific legislation compelled children to attend school, these laws were administered at the local level. It was hoped that by allowing the rules to be made close to home, the resulting legislation would be more palatable to the parents. These local regulations were a poor solution to the school attendance problem of the entire country since parents who sought to skirt local laws could easily change jobs and residences to avoid sending their children to school. Universal educational aims were not enhanced by these local plans, so eventually, national compulsory education was viewed as the only workable scheme.[2]

One overriding opinion of the classical thinkers was that if schooling were made compulsory, justice demanded that it should be made "free." A "free" school was simply a school funded entirely out of tax revenues, and devoid of student fees. The resistance of many classicals to this method of educational provision was unequivocal. They firmly adhered to free market tenets and easily concluded that the extent of government involvement in the economy and society, in general, and in education, in particular, was becoming greater than most people realized and larger than they desired. Additionally, they observed that with the gradual increase in governmental rules and regulations, private schools were finding it more and more difficult to comply with the costs of each "revised" code. Thus, the fees which private schools must charge to remain profitable while obeying the law were growing steadily. All the while the competition of "free" government schooling was becoming even stronger. Government in education was now a force to be reckoned with; once the bureaucratic administrative machinery was set into place, the provider of private education felt lucky to survive it all.

Adam Smith, the quintessential free market thinker, presented two different opinions of public involvement in education. On the one hand, he declared that "those parts of education ... for the teaching of which there are no public institutions, are generally the best taught."[3] More directly, Smith maintained that public schools were doomed to be inefficient because they operated in an environment lacking competition: "were there no public institutions for education, no sciences would be taught for which there was not some demand, or which the circumstances of the times did not render it either necessary, or convenient, or at least fashionable, to learn."[4] On the other hand, Smith acknowledged the twin problems of the dissemination of information to the masses and of assuring quality in higher education. To solve these difficulties, he presumed that state activity would be welcomed in the "erecting and maintaining ... of certain public institutions which it can never be for the interest of individuals, to erect and maintain; because the profit could neither repay the expense to any individual or small number of individuals, though it may frequently do much more than repay it to a great society."[5] However, it must be recalled that Smith repeatedly insisted that even the poorest students should be required to pay small fees for their studies, even if the buildings were provided and preserved by the state.

When analyzing the possibility of using compulsory education legislation to assure a basic level of knowledge among the masses, Smith suggested a test of comprehension rather than a school attendance law. Also, he favored a similar testing arrangement "among persons of middling or more than middling rank and fortune" to insure proficiency in "science and philosophy." One of Smith's methods of examination would entail "some sort of probation, even in the higher and more difficult sciences, to be undergone by every person before he was permitted to exercise any liberal profession, or before he could be received as a candidate for any honourable office of trust or profit."[6] Smith desired to have testing instruments give evidence of the individual's acquired knowledge; these would have more validity than certificates from educational institutions, he held.

T. R. Malthus unhesitatingly favored government interference in the world of education. He recorded that the British government had "lavished immense sums on the poor ... but in their education ... (had) been miserably deficient. It is surely a great national disgrace that the education of the lower classes of people in England should be left merely to a few Sunday schools ... ."[7] Malthus affirmed that it was the *duty* of government to supply "instruction of the people."[8] Besides a government which did not teach its citizens that they are dependent "upon themselves for the chief part of their happiness or misery" was not fulfilling its true goal.[9] Unable to think for themselves, uneducated members of society could not be depended upon to make the right social decisions. Since Malthus emphasized unceasingly that the well-being of any society was ultimately determined by the numbers of people who share in its resources, education, especially that which "lay considerable stress on the frequent explanation of the real state of the lower classes ... as affected by the principle of population," was essential to strong societal health.[10] It was chiefly government's responsibility to see that population information reached the widest range of its citizens; thus, Malthus wrote: "No government can approach to perfection that does not provide for the instruction of the people."[11]

Although Ricardo and Malthus agreed on some macroeconomic policy prescriptions, in regard to government in education, Ricardo was as opposed to it as Malthus favored it. Ricardo saw no possibility of a positive tie between government and education. Ricardo's negative reaction to government involvement in the provision of schooling was incidental to his consideration of government management of the Poor Laws. Ricardo firmly believed that the implementation of the Poor Laws was a great encouragement to population growth. He reasoned that since the government had blundered so badly at its attempts at poor relief, its interference in education could hardly be expected to be better. He asserted, "I have invariably objected to the poor laws, and to every system which should give encouragement to an excess of population. If you are to feed, clothe and educate all the children of the poor, you will be giving a great stimulus to a principle already too active."[12] Ricardo, as Malthus, was keenly aware of growing population pressures. Malthus thought education provided by government would be a cure; Ricardo thought it would be a curse.

J. B. Say took a strong progovernment stance in his thinking about education; he was as fervently for government involvement as T. R. Malthus, but he was more specific in his reasoning. Say penned this observation, "if the community wish to have the benefit of more knowledge and intelligence in the laboring classes, it must dispense it at public charge."[13] Without hesitation he identified the state as the subject of public education through "the establishment of primary schools of reading, writing, and arithmetic." Say explained that since these subjects "are the groundwork of all knowledge, ... (they) are quite sufficient for the cultivation of the lower classes."[14] The state was not only the logical provider of universal education in the basic skills, but it was also the most cost efficient provider Say held. He decided that the state would be adept at selecting the most "improved methods of mutual instruction" to help reduce the fiscal burden. Say pointed out the method touted by Bentham and Mill and preferred by Ricardo, the Lancaster method of monitorial teaching, as one which would "afford a ready and most economical means of universally diffusing knowledge amongst the inferior classes."[15] Thus, state provided Lancasterian schools would be cheap and efficient means of spreading learning to the masses Say deduced.

Yet Say proceeded toward his choice of government supply of education of the poor with caution. He warned that there was an "evil attending the productive efforts of government." As his contemporary, Adam Smith, Say acknowledged that government production "counteract(s) the individual industry ... of its competitors in production. The state is too formidable a rival ... it has too much wealth and power at its command."[16] He, too, feared the destruction of the system of private education because of its inability to compete with the overwhelming amount of public resources devoted to governmentally provided instruction. Say detailed his thoughts: " ... care must be taken, that encouragement of one branch shall not operate to discourage another. This is the general mischief of premiums awarded by the public; a private teacher or institution will not be adequately paid, where the same kind of instruction is to be had for nothing, though, perhaps from inferior teachers."[17] He voiced the concern expressed by Smith and repeated by subsequent thinkers that a lower quality service with a zero price may be preferred (especially by the nondiscriminating) to a better quality service with any positive price. The government could easily eliminate the demand for private educational services when this occurred, Say concluded. Consequently, Say favored government in education but desired to limit government's role. Government education of the poor was acceptable in his view, but beyond basic provision, Say sought a system that preserved the principle of market supply.

In this regard Say specified the crippling effects of public provision of education on the suppliers of the service. Without the actions of the free market as a guide, he feared that "talent may be superceded by mediocrity; and a check given to private exertions."[18] Say advocated a system of private and public education existing side by side. The loss of private sources of schooling would be deplorable, Say opined, since private education yielded benefits to the society as a whole that were "incalcuable."

Frenchman Claude Frederic Bastiat looked at education after the French Revolution had provided the French government with the opportunity to try its hand at educational control. When Bastiat wrote, the despotism of Napoleon had altered the position of government involvement in French education; it had changed from a situation of benign neglect to one of total entanglement. The first fallacy of socially provided education which Bastiat found in the French system was the delusion of "free" education.[19] He asked, "Can the state make instruction shine down, like the light of day on every corner of the land without requiring any effort from anybody?"[20] Bastiat wondered if the rational people of France had stopped to consider that "public services cost everybody something. The reason they cost the receiver nothing is that everybody has paid for them in advance."[21] He continued that since the taxpayers have already paid for state education, naturally they would be adverse to paying for private education. Thus the total contribution of government education to national produce was zero since "public service replaces private service. It adds nothing to the nation's general industry or to its wealth."[22]

Bastiat delved deeper into the idea of the state in education by questioning if government involvement were even necessary. He inquired of those who championed state education, "Will it be alleged that education is so universally necessary that we are permitted for its sake to compromise with justice our principles?"[23] Bastiat persisted, "There is nothing the state cannot give gratis if we follow this line of reasoning; ... gratuitous food as well, and gratuitous clothing, and gratuitous housing, etc."[24] He alleged that since food was even more important than education, the state would also be obliged to furnish it as well as everything else that the public needed to survive.

Bastiat decried the fact that publicly provided education placed such restrictions on individual freedom that it influenced the whole human character: "The individual is no longer free to buy what he wishes, when he wishes, to consult his means, his convenience, his situation, his tastes, his moral standards." [25] Once the individual was relieved of the responsibility for satisfying his own wants, he ceased to concern himself with doing so: "he loses the habit of judging for himself." [26] Bastiat was firmly convinced that "for man, responsibility is everything! (Without it) he falls into inertia and no longer counts except as a unit of the herd." [27] Mankind could never progress without individuality; in fact, Bastiat expected that it would even be hard to survive without it, since uniformity "atrophies the noblest faculties of human nature." [28] Finally, Bastiat lamented that individuals lost their ability to think clearly when they were faced with government involvement in all things: "they have been told so many times that all religion, all wisdom, all knowledge, all enlightenment, all morality reside in the state or are derived from the state" that they are unable to exert any individual judgment. [29] Education which was supposed to bring out the leadership qualities in men, under government became the suppressor of the human spirit.

Not only did Bastiat question the state's right to provide education, he also disputed its ability to do so. It was easy for the state to "forcibly exact ... remuneration from citizens and then distribute the type of instruction it prefers without asking them for a second payment," Bastiat discovered. [30] But he deplored the quality of instruction that any government would supply; practically, he recorded that "education by a governmental power ... is education by a political party, by a sect momentarily triumphant." It stood to reason that state education could not be impartial, Bastiat decided, because "it is education on behalf of one idea, of one system, to the exclusion of all others." [31] Therefore, government education was necessarily biased and could not possibly teach students objectively.

Bastiat had argued that the provision of education by the state through taxation was not only costly, confining and biased, but it was also unjust. This occurred because "those who do not learn pay for those who do; those who learn little for those who learn much; those who are preparing for trades for those who will enter the professions." [32] The inequity of this system might be extremely severe, as in the case of a man who "does not have enough bread to satisfy his hunger, and yet the government takes from him part of his bread which would be indispensable to him, in order to give him instruction ... that he neither needs or desires." [33] In Bastiat's mind the alternatives for the state were clear: "It can permit this transaction of teaching-and-learning to operate fully, and without the use of force, or it can force human wills in this matter by taking from some of them enough to pay the teachers who are appointed by the government to instruct others, without charge."[34] Bastiat was unyielding about the consequences of government adopting the second case: the government "commits legal plunder by violating (the) liberty and property" of its citizens.[35]

Jeremy Bentham, a man with pretentious plans for profitable private education, often pictured the economic inefficiencies and financial wastes which were by-products of the state control of instruction. But Bentham had to acknowledge the special qualities of educational supply which limited its revenue generating ability. Perhaps because of his own futile attempts at creating a system of education that would yield sufficient reward to investors, Bentham finally concluded: "There should be government activity in everything connected with the propagation of knowledge - universities, schools, agricultural and scientific research and the collection of statistics."[36] However, Bentham would not rule out private provision of these studies as a supplement to a governmental foundation.

Wilhelm von Humboldt, who was directly involved with state education as Minister of Worship and Public Instruction in Prussia, foresaw far worse dangers than most of the other classicals to government interaction in schooling. Humboldt was the architect of the Prussian education system and the founder of the University of Berlin but his doubts about the value of public activity in instruction had begun early in his own education.[37] In general, Humboldt was apprehensive about growing government activity in all areas of society. He was firmly convinced that in a community filled with state agencies and state institutions "men are neglected for things, and creative powers for results."[38] The political community thus described becomes "living but lifeless." This type of system contrasted with Humboldt's strong belief in "Bildung," the fullest, richest, and most harmonious development of the potentialities of the individual, the community, and the human race. State organizations produced uniformity, weakened the vitality of the nation, and deprived men of freedom of choice, he decided. Also, he judged that "Whatever does not spring from a man's free choice ... remains alien to his true nature."[39] All of these shortcomings were particularly hazardous to the instruction of youth, Humboldt felt. If there were one occupation which demanded energy and innovation, it was teaching.

Humboldt wrote from an awkward position: philosophically he was opposed to state education, but practically he was the director of a state educational system. He once remarked that "national education seems to me to lie wholly beyond the limits within which the State's activity should properly be confirmed."[40] Even the good that did come from public involvement, he recorded, was in spite of, not because of, the public presence. Humboldt warned: " ... government must always remain conscious that it really neither brings about such results, however desirable, nor can it bring them about. It must remember, in fact, that its intervention is invariably an obstruction to attaining the desired results, that everything would proceed infinitely better without its help."[41] Humboldt sought a fundamentally private system of universal education, with a minimum amount of government aid.

With these feelings about government and its presence in education, how was it that Humboldt could and did bring about such sweeping reforms in the German educational system? During a large part of his life, Humboldt was a career diplomat who served his country abroad; yet he was always more at home with philosophy than with practical matters. Although Humboldt disdained the value structure of the average German politician, he was quick to sense where the power lay.[42] When offered the opportunity to reconstruct the university after the Napoleonic invasion, he seized the chance to implement his philosophy of higher education. In the articles of incorporation of the University of Berlin, he emphasized that, by design, the school focused on advances in truth and science. Additionally, he demanded that the university be built on *Lehrfreiheit* and *Lernfreiheit* which was "the right of the teachers to teach and students to learn whatever the love of truth urged."[43] Humboldt earnestly desired to create a system of higher education which would serve as a model for all of Europe. If it were through government that he had to work, Humboldt was enough of a pragmatist to accept government's aid to achieve his goal.

James Mill had spent the better part of this life experimenting with various types of privately provided education. In a manner similar to Humboldt, his philosophical leanings were plainly toward social systems structured around freedom and flexibility. Mill concluded from his investigations that universal nonsectarian education in basic skills could be provided cheaply enough using the monitorial method to be financed by voluntary contributions especially in rural areas. Among the pieces of supporting evidence for Mill's claim was Malthus' description of the Norway plan which furnished educational basics for all children all of one religion adequately and cheaply. For the children of families with sufficient income, Mill recommended schools like Bentham's Chrestomathia. These schools could maintain themselves through subscription and student fees. Even though he preferred private education, when pressed, Mill could not overrule the possibility of government aid to universal education for the masses if private funds were found to be deficient. Mill penned his opinion of state education for those in need in the *Edinburgh Review* of February 1813:

> ... if their education be entrusted to

Government, or to persons patronized by the Government, - we can only say, that although we are far from considering the danger either small or chimerical, it is still so very great and good to have the whole facility of reading and writing diffused through the whole body of the people, that we should be willing to run considerable risks for its acquirement, or even greatly to accelerate that acquirement.[44]

Quizically, Mill was willing to sacrifice even his faith in the Principles of Association for state provision of basic education. He judged that primary education was so important to life that "it is scarcely possible for any government to convert (it) into (an) instrument of evil ... ." Mill thought that government provided instruction would yield a net benefit: "the impressions, indeed, which it is impossible to make at the early age at which reading and writing are taught, and during the very short time that teaching lasts, are so very slight and transitory, that they must be easily effaced whenever there is anything to counteract them."[45] Mill calculated the age for elementary education to be those very young years before apprenticeship could begin. As Smith and Bentham, he felt that this was the most practical time to educate pauper children since it minimized the amount of interference with their income earning ability. Mill decided that any harm which would result from government involvement in this type of education would only be of an extremely limited nature.

The recipient of an intense dose of James Mill's educational philosophy and methodology, John Stuart Mill, perceived government intervention in education as somewhat better than a last resort. J. S. Mill argued that the voluntary principle was wholly inadequate for the dissemination of basic knowledge to the masses. He summoned government to meet the educational needs of its citizens "by supplying elementary schools" or "by giving pecuniary support to elementary schools."[46] Mill's intent was clearly to have the state provide enough financial aid to make schooling "accessible to all the children of the poor, either freely, or for a payment too inconsiderable to be felt."[47]

Mill advocated the interjection of government into the realm of education both in practice and in principle. Practically, the financial needs of mass education precluded voluntary contributions; following his convictions, Mill decided that since "the uncultivated cannot be competent judges of cultivation, ... education ... is one of those things which is admissible in principle that government should provide for the people."[48] Mill did not have much faith in the ability of the worker to pull himself up from his oppressed condition. Without the stimulus of government, the masses would stand by idly while educational

125

opportunities went untouched. Mill considered that "all instruction which is given, not that we may live, but that we may live well; all which aims at making us wise or good, calls for the care of government" because "the majority have neither the desire nor sufficient notion of the means, of becoming much wiser or better than they are."[49] Mill was so taken with the lack of desire for education on the part of the laborer that he candidly concluded: "It is therefore an allowable exercise of the powers of government to impose on parents the legal obligation of giving elementary instruction to children."[50]

Mill was quick to demonstrate that neither government supply of elementary education nor compulsory education laws conflicted with the concept of personal freedom. He claimed that "when the government provides means for filling a certain end, leaving individuals free to avail themselves of different means if their opinion preferable, there is no infringement of liberty."[51] In fact Mill thought that the only way to guarantee a country's future freedom was through the swift spread of basic learning. Maintaining that education was a prerequisite to citizen participation and that active citizen participation was crucial to a vigorous economy, Mill *demanded* a literate populace. He was intensely optimistic about the future condition of society when universal education was commonplace:

> Very few years of a real working-class representation would have passed over our heads before there would be in every parish a school rate, and the school doors freely open to all the world; and in one generation from that time England would be an educated nation.[52]

As much as Mill desired government activity as a catalyst to the diffusion of knowledge, he still harbored a fear of allowing the state to become involved with the spread of ideas. The peril of state schools was "that most fatal one of tending to be all alike; to form the same unvarying habits of mind and turn of character."[53] When the state had control of education, it had ultimate domination of the minds of its citizens; Mill wrote:

> A general State education is a mere contrivance for molding people to be exactly like one another; and as the mold in which it casts them is that which pleases the predominant power in the government in proportion as it is efficient and successful, it establishes a despotism over the mind leading by natural tendency over the body.[54]

Because of the strength that government could wield once it

regulated schooling, Mill was fiercely opposed to a state monopoly in education. Mill recalled the French experience for an example of monopoly education: although the students may learn more, they are inferior to the English "in the love and practice of personal and political freedom." [55] Mill made his strongest plea for the protection of human individuality. His fear of state control over the human mind through education was evident in this statement: "It is not endurable that a government should, either *de iure* or *de facto*, have a complete control over the education of the people ... . A government which can move the opinions and sentiments of the people from their youth upwards can do with them whatever it pleases." [56] Mill expected that compulsory education laws combined with a Parliamentary grant system of educational finance which permitted variety to flourish in the school system would produce universal education with the lowest cost to personal freedom.

Herbert Spencer championed the cause of individuality. Unlike Mill, he judged that compulsory education legislation and state interference in educational supply would definitely eradicate the unique elements which each individual person possessed. Spencer viewed the education problem from a special vantage point, the end of the nineteenth century. Most of the other classical writers recorded their thoughts in anticipation of change; Spencer had witnessed the changes in government education over half a century. If he had ever favored state involvement, his attitude had become dramatically altered by the exponential growth of state action in education. Spencer was convinced that an uncontrollable force had been unleashed against an unwitting society:

> On the day when £30,000 (1833) a year in aid of education was voted as an experiment, the name of idiot would have been given to an opponent who prophesied that in fifty years the sum spent through imperial taxes and local rates would amount to £10,000,000 (1890), or who said that the aid to education would be followed by aids to feeding and clothing, or who said that parents and children, alike deprived of all opinion, would even if starving, be compelled by fine or imprisonment to conform, and receive that which, with papal assumption, the State calls education. No one, I say, would have dreamt that out of so innocent-looking a germ would have so quickly evolved this tyrannical system, tamely submitted to by people who fancy themselves free.[57]

In a line of thought reminiscent of the freedom-loving Bastiat, Spencer reasoned that when the state had the "duty" of

127

providing intellectual food, it would soon assume the duty of supplying material food as well, and would in the extreme, insist upon furnishing total care for all children.[58]   Spencer envisioned no limits to state growth until the family was replaced by the state and a socialist society with "community care of offspring" was established.[59]   The elimination of state involvement in education was a necessary first step to forestall the inevitable progression toward socialism in Spencer's opinion.

Since uniformity within a system reduced administrative problems, Spencer asserted that state managed education would naturally tend toward as little diversity as possible.[60]   Once in place, the state institutions would become changeless.   Spencer concluded that the roots of state institutions were in the past and the present, never in the future.   A state network of uniform, inflexible schools was the best that government could give, since government measured its success in the ability to maintain the status quo, not in the ability to change it.   Spencer remarked how inappropriate this way of thinking was to education which "properly, so called, is closely associated with change, is its pioneer, is the never sleeping agent of revolution, is always fitting men for higher things and unfitting them for things as they are."[61]   For Spencer the very essence of education clashed powerfully with the nature of the state.

Spencer took on a Ricardian tone when he noted that what state education would do was to reduce the level of parental responsibility and thereby foster population growth.   Freed from the financial concern of supplying education to their offspring, even prudent individuals would be encouraged to marry earlier.[62] Spencer summarized his feelings: "The more the state undertakes to do for his family, the more are the expenses of the married man reduced, at the cost of the unmarried man, and the greater becomes the temptation to marry."   Government meddling in the lives of individuals through education will not strengthen them, but will cause them to become irresponsible and dependent, Spencer concluded; he wrote "government can confer knowledge only at the expense of character."[63]

Since Spencer questioned even the need for state uniformly provided education which he considered a restraint on individuality, he was decidedly opposed to compulsory education.   He recoiled at the commonly accepted idea that the "state must not simply educate (the laboring classes) but must force education upon them."[64]   Spencer emphasized the irony of coercive education.   Using "brute force for educational purposes" could never achieve the goals of education because "education has for its object the formation of character ... so as finally to develop the child into a man of well-proportioned and harmonious nature."[65] Spencer reasoned that to subject an individual to compulsion in order to teach him about freedom and harmony was absurd. He penned: "Contrasting the means to be employed with the work to be done, we are at once struck with their utter unfitness. Instead of creating a new internal state which shall exhibit itself in better deeds, coercion can manifestly do nothing but forcibly mold externals into a coarse semblance of such a state. In the family as in society, it can simply restrain; it cannot educate."[66]

Inasmuch as Spencer asserted that state education was both fruitless and unnecessary, he deduced that taxes levied for this purpose were unjust. He wrote of the personal injustice involved: "I should deny the equity of taking, through the rates, the earnings of A to pay for the teaching the children of B."[67] Society, as a whole, suffered a more fundamental injustice, he felt, since government encroached upon personal liberty by using tax money to pay for these unnecessary educational services: "Inasmuch as the taking away, by government, of more than a man's property than is needful for maintaining his rights is an infringement of his rights and therefore a reversal of the government's function toward him, and inasmuch as the taking away of his property to educate his own or other people's children is not needful for the maintaining of his rights, the taking away of his property for such a purpose is wrong."[68]

In contrast McCulloch could find no injustice in the use of general public revenues for educational purposes. Indeed, he claimed the government had not used enough revenue to support education and was not fulfilling "one of its most pressing duties" that of providing "elementary instruction for all classes."[69] McCulloch was blind to any detriments that this particular government expenditure would have on society; "there cannot be the shadow of a doubt that, were government to interfere as far as to cause a public school to be established in every parish in England, where the fees should be moderate, and where really useful instruction should be communicated to the scholars, its interference would be the highest degree beneficial."[70]

Although McCulloch advocated government spending on education, he thought a good deal more must be done by all suppliers of education before an efficient national educational program would be in effect. Moreover, he stressed the need for all types of supply, not only government aid: "And though much has been done to supply this deficiency by benevolent individuals and societies, and more recently by government, a great deal remains to be accomplished, both as respects the diffusion of instruction, and the improvement of its quality."[71] McCulloch emphasized that one means of assuring educational quality under any system was to charge modest fees. As classicals before him, he believed in "a paid and therefore a prized education."[72]

Nassau Senior and John Stuart Mill held similar views on the role of government in the society. Senior's opinion of government's place is best described by his words: "The only rational foundation of government ... is expediency ... the general benefit of the community. It is the duty of a Government to do whatever is conducive to the welfare of the governed." [73] However, Senior's pure laissez-faire sentiments could not hold firm in the face of what he saw in the streets. The conditions in the London slums would not be changed adhering to a laissez-faire philosophy of government. Sounding very much like Mill, Senior noted that "it is only the educated who are aware that education is necessary." [74] The welfare of those who would not ever voluntarily demand education, a group that Senior supposed was "to be counted not by hundreds but by hundreds of thousands," was the responsibility of the "higher classes, (standing) in *loco parentis*." [75] The poorer classes were totally dependent upon the upper classes, their "usefulness or mischievousness," their "happiness or misery," all were a function of "the education given them by the State" in the name of the higher classes. Senior did not doubt that the "welfare of the governed" was immeasurably enhanced by this government action.

Senior sympathized with the choices low income working parents had to make when faced with the high opportunity costs for their children's schooling. These parents were not irresponsible, only poor, Senior thought. Poor parents faced conflicting responsibilities: "it is the duty of every man to provide education for his children; ... it is also his duty to provide for them all the other necessaries. These expenses are ... constant ...; they cannot be omitted for a day." [76] Senior maintained that there could be no choice between payments for food or shelter and payments for education and even the most well-intentioned laborer may have to forego an individual child's education to ensure the survival of the entire family. As Mill, Senior envisioned temporary government aid to the uneducated to encourage them to educate their children: "We may look forward to the time when the labouring classes shall possess the means, the intelligence, and the conscientiousness which will enable and induce them to give their children a good education. But that time has not yet come." [77] Government aid to education was clearly needed for the children of the laboring class, as well as for those in abject poverty. Senior had come to the conclusion that working parents might know the value of education for their children but might be unable to pay the price. Government help would enable these parents to afford education. However, Senior definitely placed a time limit on government involvement. As one generation was given basic literacy under the guiding hand of government, their children would be more willing and able to educate their own offspring without government interference. Senior looked forward to "the time when the labouring

130

population may be safely entrusted with the education of their children."[78] Senior expected education to cause increases in individual living standards; also, as family income rose, children's wages became relatively less important to sustenance. At that time, the state could remove its school aid and allow the supply of education to return to the private sector where Senior believed it belonged.

From a contrasting point of view, Karl Marx placed the state in the philosophical heart of education. In his earliest works he identified the state as a philosophical teacher. For Marx, the state was a "true educational institution" and it "educates its members by making them part of the state."[79] These Marxian remarks were distinctly similar to the Millian concepts of "political education" and "active participatory government." Furthermore, Marx credited the state with the power to transform individuals into social beings possessing "universal aims." When an individual found "his satisfaction in the life of the whole," then, Marx judged, he would be on the road to "spiritual freedom."[80] The macroeconomic benefits of the state in education had never been so strongly expressed by the classicals. In sum, Marx believed that education by the state, as a representative of societal authority, was a certain route to social cohesion and the maximization of social welfare.

Years passed and Marx witnessed a huge disparity between the ideal education and the actual education offered to the workers of his day. Part of the difference was due to the activity of the state itself. Although he and Engles had repeated the same educational prescription for decades, their plan was continually misconstrued. In *Critique of the Gotha Program*, Marx examined the outline sent to him for his comments by the German workers' party. Part of the party platform read: "Universal and *equal elementary education* by the state. Universal compulsory school attendance. Free instruction."[81] Marx was decidedly against the entire program but found its educational provisions particularly distasteful. He queried: "*Equal elementary education*?" What idea lies behind these words?" Marx patiently explained that for equality in education to be achieved in "present-day-society," the upper classes would have to "be compulsorily reduced to the modicum of education - the elementary school. For only then would there be true educational equality with the wage-workers and the peasants as well."[82]

Marx also had problems accepting the Gotha Program's demand for "universal compulsory school attendance" and "free instruction." He pointed out that "the former exists even in Germany; the second in Switzerland and in the United States in the case of elementary schools. If in some states of the latter country higher educational institutions are also 'free' that only

131

means in fact defraying the cost of the education of the upper classes from the general tax receipts."[83] Marx objected to the use of ambiguous socialistic slogans in an outline which was proposed as a blueprint for the future of society. He hoped the party members could generate some specific educational plans to stand behind their lofty social goals. To get them started in the right direction, Marx offered advice to make the educational program more viable for a changing society: "the paragraph on the schools should have at least demanded technical schools (theoretical and practical) in combination with the elementary schools."[84] To the end, Marx trusted technical education with the keys to the new social order.

In *Critique of the Gotha Program*, Marx reiterated his grave disappointment with the type of education supplied for the worker in a capitalist state. He stated flatly that "elementary education by the state is altogether objectionable." He equated contemporary state interference in education with church interference, concluding that "government and church should rather be equally excluded from any influence on the school." Marx employed an idea he had expressed long before when he asserted, "the state had need, on the contrary, of a very stern education by the people."[85] To Marx, education dominated by a bourgeoisie-run state was almost worse than no education at all. Marx had seen a change in the educational provision of his day: the state's position in German education was growing stronger and stronger, even as it strayed further and further away from its role of philosophic teacher.

Henry Fawcett, who was in agreement with many of Marx's ideas concerning the nature of education, slipped back into the bosom of the early classical political economists when he discussed the place of the state in education. He fixed state provided education squarely in the category of poor relief, as Ricardo had done. Fawcett demanded that the appropriate personal disgrace should be attached to educational relief, since it was no different from the relief given for the provision of other necessities. He thought that the stigma of pauperism belonged to those who could not or would not pay a few pence a week for their children's education. Furthermore, Fawcett, in a manner similar to Bastiat and Malthus, considered the twin consequences of state supply of education to be financial injustice and moral inequity. First, he considered the school taxes themselves unfair because those who did not have any children paid the school rates, and the parents with two children paid education taxes for the parents with fourteen children. Second, he (and Mrs. Fawcett) were abashed at the reduction in moral responsibility which relief payments encouraged; they penned to the *London Times* in December 1870, "It seems to be considered that the reward of restraint and prudence should be a heavy fine to defray the cost of self-

132

indulgence and improvidence of others."[86]

Moreover, Fawcett questioned the assumption that education was as necessary as food or clothes, or that the child suffered irreparable damage from lack of it. Therefore, Fawcett, as Spencer, viewed compulsory education as a fundamental reduction in personal liberty and was very hesitant to suggest it without strong reason. Furthermore, Fawcett believed that the issue of legal compulsion would be meaningless within a few generations, since schooling would gradually become a deeply rooted social habit. Looking toward a brighter future filled with educated citizens, he penned, "Education begets education, because people who have enjoyed its advantages will strive hard to let their children enjoy them also."[87] In a manner similar to John Stuart Mill and Senior, Fawcett held that compulsory education laws would be short term policy suggestions.

The last of the classical political economists, Henry Sidgwick, investigated the issue of state action in education. His thoughts were a blend of the ideas of the classical writers with liberal inclinations. Sidgwick proposed state intervention in education and compulsory education laws based on the arguments of paternalism and distributive justice. He considered the "education as a social good argument" a weaker defense for public educational supply. Additionally, the financial difficulties of providing quality education to the masses made state furnished educational aid more appealing, Sidgwick reasoned. Therefore, as a practical man Sidgwick championed government involvement in education, but with restraint. Sidgwick realized that feelings of social inbalance were growing too strong to be ignored: "The enlarged conception of social and political duty which is now prevalent is impelling us with increasing force to promote positively the attainment of a good life for all."[88] Government would be the logical source for providing the means to achieve large and swift increases in social welfare. But Sidgwick, reared in the classical economic tradition of government was as cautious as Senior and Mill: he hoped that solutions to the problems which accompanied the enrichment of the lives of the masses would be "through the action of the State, so far as experience shows this to be prudent, but also through private and voluntarily associated effort, outside and apart from or in co-operation with, government."[89] Even though classical free market thinking was still the focus of his economic philosophy, Sidgwick knew that flexibility was the key to an uncertain future.

Sidgwick stressed the paternalistic intervention of government. He echoed the Millian idea that men might be misled regarding the amount of education that was best for their children. Therefore, he concluded that a minimum level of education could be compelled by law. Sidgwick argued that if paternalism necessitated compulsion, then equity demanded that public funds be collected to help defray the expenses of compliance with this law. This parallels the thought expressed by several of the classical economists from the time of James Mill onwards, that if something is made compulsory, it should be made "free." Sidgwick even declared that without government financial aid compulsory universal education would be meaningless: "the expense of this education, if not artificially reduced by pecuniary aid from Government, would ... be so serious a burden on the poorest class, that it would be practically impossible to make the compulsion universal."[90] Carrying his discussion of justice in compulsory education further, he specified the kinds of things that should be included in the curriculum: the instruction "should be strictly confined to imparting aptitudes of incontestable utility to industry." This was just, Sidgwick wrote, because "whatever is made universally obligatory to acquire should ... be universally useful."[91] Paternalism necessitated compulsory education legislation; compulsory school laws made state financial aid and state determination of curriculum essential.

Sidgwick's second argument for universal "free" education was on the basis of distributive justice. In this discussion, he held that the provider of the service was not in question. He recorded that if it is the desire of the citizens of a country to remove "all removable differences in remuneration that are due to causes other than the voluntary exertions of the labourers," then the means of training the workers must be brought within the reach of all classes "by a well organized system of free education."[92] Only through education could inequities in income distribution be cured; only government could supply an educational system appropriate to the task. Continuing this thought, Sidgwick suggested "a division of cost between local and general taxation" since although the benefits of education were diffused throughout the community, some localities benefited more than others.[93]

Sidgwick's main reasons for suggesting government in education were to protect innocent children from ignorant parents, the paternalistic argument, and to foster equity in income distribution, the distributive justice argument. However, he could not completely neglect the social goods defense of government in education. Sidgwick had decided that all taxpayers were net beneficiaries of the macroeconomic spillovers from education; he did not see rampant injustice perpetrated through the use of taxes for educational purposes. Sidgwick calculated that the "persons taxed gain indirectly private advantages of some sort worth purchasing at the price they are compelled to pay."[94] He classified elementary education as a good with a large macroeconomic spillover effect and maintained that means of provision other than the state were difficult or awkward. Sidgwick was led

134

to the conclusion that in many ways social provision of education was advantageous to society. Nevertheless, Sidgwick, as a true classical economist, was compelled to warn of the dangers in accepting government help without due caution. He believed that inviting the government to become involved in education was "a question which involves a very difficult and complex comparison of various kinds of social utility." Sidgwick freely admitted that "the balance of advantages in any case must depend very largely on particular circumstances and varying social conditions."[95] Once again Sidgwick was displaying his open-mindedness about choosing solutions to the problems of the upcoming century. New times will demand new tools, Sidgwick believed; a different role for government within a traditionally free society might certainly be possible.

NOTES

1. See: Henry Roper, "Toward an Elementary Education Act for England and Wales, 1865-1868," *British Journal of Educational Studies*, Vol. 23 (2), pp. 181-205.

2. See: W. H. G. Armytage, *Four Hundred Years of English Education* (Cambridge, 1970), pp. 137-153.

3. Adam Smith, *An Inquiry into the Nature and Causes of the Wealth of Nations*, ed. Edwin Cannan (New York, 1937), p. 253.

4. Ibid., p. 753.

5. Quoted in E. G. West, *Adam Smith* (New Rochelle, N. Y., 1969), p. 179.

6. Quoted in Joseph Spengler "Adam Smith on Human Capital," *The American Economic Review*, Vol. 67 (1), p. 35.

7. Quoted in Pierre N. V. Tu, "The Classical Economists and Education," *Kyklos*, Vol. 22, p. 695.

8. T. R. Malthus, *An Essay on the Principle of Population*, 3rd ed. (London, 1806), p. 423.

9. Ibid., p. 415.

10. Ibid.

11. Ibid., p. 423.

12. David Ricardo, *The Works and Correspondence of David Ricardo*, ed. Piero Sraffa (Cambridge, 1952), Vol. VII, pp. 359-360.

13. J. B. Say, *A Treatise on Political Economy* (New York, 1964), p. 435.

14. Ibid.

15. Ibid., p. 436.

16. Ibid., p. 200.

17. Ibid., p. 437.

18. Ibid.

19. E. G. West recorded in 1976 sentiments which are reminiscent of Bastiat: "A tradition of 'free' public schools is a tradition of disguise, obscurantism, and ambiguity, as indicated by the need to use quotation marks around the word 'free';" in *Nonpublic School Aid* (Lexington, Massachusetts, 1976), p. 90.

20. Frederic Bastiat, *Economic Harmonies*, ed. George B. deHuszar (New York, 1964), p. 235.

21. Ibid., p. 450.

22. Ibid.

23. Ibid., p. 235.

24. Ibid.

25. Ibid., p. 450.

26. Ibid.

27. Ibid., p. 452.

28. Ibid., p. 451.

29. Ibid., p. 453-454.

30. Ibid., p. 235.

31. Frederic Bastiat, *Selected Essays on Political Economy*, ed. George B. deHuszar (New York, 1964), p. 280.

32. Bastiat, *Economic Harmonies*, p. 235.

33. Ibid., p. 450.

34. Frederic Bastiat, *The Law* (Irvington-on-Hudson, New York, 1962), p. 31.

35. Ibid.

36. Quoted in Samuel Hollander, "The Role of the State in Vocational Training: the Classical Economists' View," *Southern Economic Journal*, Vol. 34, p. 519.

37. See Paul R. Sweet, *Wilhelm von Humboldt: A Biography*, 1767-1808 (Columbus, Ohio, 1978), Vol. I, p. 84.

38. Wilhelm von Humboldt, *The Limits of State Action*, ed. J. W. Burrow (Cambridge, 1969), p. 35.

39. Ibid., p. 28.

40. Ibid., p. 54.

41. Wilhelm von Humboldt, *Humanist Without Portfolio: An Anthology of the Writings of Wilhelm von Humboldt* (Wayne State University Press, 1963), p. 133.

42. Sweet, p. 256.

43. See: Val Gendron, *The Dragon Tree* (New York, 1961, p. 133.

44. James Mill, *On Education*, ed. W. H. Burston (Cambridge, 1969), p. 32.

45. Ibid.

46. See: Hollander, p. 522.

47. Ibid.

48. John Stuart Mill, *Principles of Political Economy*, ed. William Ashley (Fairfield, 1976), p. 953-954.

49. Quoted in John M. Robson, *The Improvement of Mankind* (London, 1968), p. 211.

50. Mill, *Principles*, p. 954.

51. Ibid., p. 943.

52. Quoted in Robson, p. 260.

53. Ibid., p. 210.

54. John Stuart Mill, *On Liberty*, ed. Currin V. Shields (New York, 1956), p. 129.

55. Edward Alexander, *Mathew Arnold and John Stuart Mill* (New York, 1965), p. 222.

56. Mill, *Principles*, p. 950.

57. Herbert Spencer, *The Man versus the State* (Caldwell, Idaho, 1965), p. 68; see, also, p. 29.

58. Herbert Spencer, *Social Statics* (New York, 1954), p. 296.

59. Herbert Spencer, *The Principles of Sociology* (New York, 1923), p. 718.

60. Spencer, *Social Statics*, p. 304.

61. Ibid., p. 305.

62. Modern writer James Buchanan opined: "In a frontier society, with population scarcity, there may well exist positive externalities from child producing that more than offset the costs of public education. In such a setting the tradition of the 'free public school', and the implicit structure of rights involved, might have possessed some efficiency justification. In a mature society ... the positive externalities seem to be non-existent," in West, *Nonpublic School Aid*, p. 120.

63. Herbert Spencer, *The Study of Sociology* (Ann Arbor, 1961), p. 316-317.

64. Spencer, *Man versus State*, p. 55.

65. Spencer, *Social Statics*, p. 161.

66. Ibid., p. 163.

67. Herbert Spencer, *Facts and Comments* (New York, 1902), pp. 83-84.

68. Spencer, *Social Statics*, p. 295.

69. Quoted in Tu, p. 700.

70. D. P. O'Brien, *J. R. McCulloch* (London, 1970), p. 344.

71. Quoted in Hollander, p. 522.

72. O'Brien, *J. R. McCulloch*, p. 344.

73. Marian Bowley, *Nassau W. Senior and Classical Economics* (Chicago, 1937), p. 265. J. S. Mill employed a "universal rule" to limit the interference of government: "the simple and vague one, that it should be admitted but when the case of expedience is strong," *Principles*, p. 800.

74. Nassau W. Senior, *Suggestions on Popular Education* (London, 1861), p. 74.

75. Ibid.

76. Nassau W. Senior, *Industrial Efficiency and Social Economy*, ed. S. Leon Levy (New York, 1928), p. 334.

77. Ibid., p. 333.

78. Ibid., p. 336.

79. Karl Marx and Friedrich Engles, *Collected Works* (New York, 1975), Vol. I, p. 193.

80. Ibid.

81. Karl Marx, *Critique of the Gotha Program* (Moscow, 1971), p. 27.

82. Ibid.

83. Ibid., pp. 27-28.

84. Ibid., p. 28.

85. Ibid.

86. Henry Sidgwick, *Pauperism: Its Causes and Remedies* (New York, 1871), p. 63.

87. Ibid., p. 124.

88. Henry Sidgwick, *Practical Ethics* (London, 1909), p. 207.

89. Ibid.

90. Henry Sidgwick, *Principles of Political Economy* (London, 1883), p. 465.

91. Ibid.
92. Ibid., p. 530.
93. Ibid., p. 558.
94. Ibid., p. 424.
95. Ibid., p. 539.

CHAPTER VIII

THE INFLUENCE OF THE CLASSICAL POLITICAL ECONOMISTS IN EDUCATIONAL ECONOMICS TODAY

THE CONTEMPORARY VIEW

At least a century has passed since most of the classical political economists recorded their opinions of education and educational supply. There have been changes in the educational environment over the years but little change has occurred in the way mainstream economists think about the place of education in the macroeconomy or the role of the government as a provider of educational services.

What do today's economists write about education? Generally, education is treated as a prime example of market failure in microeconomic analysis. Campbell R. McConnell presents a clear explanation of education as a good with significant spillover benefits in his widely used principles of economics text. He writes: "But education also confers sizable benefits upon society; for example, the economy as a whole benefits from a more versatile and more productive labor force, on the one hand, and smaller outlays in the areas of crime prevention, law enforcement, and welfare programs, on the other. Significant, too, is the fact that political participation correlates positively with the level of education; for example, the percentage of persons who vote increases with educational attainment."[1] Education, therefore, is a good to be sought for its social, as well as its private benefits.[2]

Additionally, contemporary economists consider the place of education in determining income. It is often repeated in current economic texts that there is a strong relationship between people with more education and people with higher incomes. Studies have shown that the marginal returns from additional schooling are highest in the primary school years.[3] This means that the most basic education, reading, writing, and simple arithmetic, brings the greatest change in individual earnings.[4] Hence, it is reasoned that one method of reducing income disparities is through the provision of universal basic skills instruction.

A third concept of education in today's economic thinking revolves around the idea of education as an investment in human capital. Heilbronner and Thurow hold that education teaches general skills which can be called "human capital." They continue, "Equally valuable is its teaching of behavior expected in high-level occupations: how to speak politely, how to be punctual, how to relate to authority, and other often overlooked attributes of classroom discipline that prepare us for jobs."[5]

141

Also, Byrnes and Stone note that workers in an educated society are more productive (because of the human capital investment) and these "more productive workers expand average standards of living by the extra output their higher productivity provides."[6] Thus the whole capital base of the society rises, increasing its ability to produce national output.

Finally, the belief that children have a natural right to education even appears in a modern economic principles presentation. This particular argument also includes the notion that parents are not able to judge the correct quantity (or quality) of education for their offspring. Lipsey, Steiner, and Purvis observe: "In an unhindered free market, the adults in a household would usually decide how much education to buy for their children. Selfish parents might buy no education, while egalitarian parents might buy the same quantity for all their children regardless of their ability."[7] The implication clearly is that, if left unguided, parents are prone to educational error.

What solutions do contemporary economic authors propose to the problems associated with education? There are several suggestions. One group of authors hold that society ought to interfere in the educational decision to protect the child and "to insure that some of the scarce educational resources are distributed according to intelligence rather than wealth."[8] In this case, the government would force parents to provide some minimum level of education for their children and would support the educational advance of lower income gifted students through public universities, scholarships, and other kinds of financial help. The usual recommendations for government action in education are those which are typically made for the provision of goods with spillover benefits. The simplest possible government spillover policy is to force individuals through legislation to do something which they would not ordinarily do. A second policy, government subsidies, relies on incentives to induce individuals to act in a certain way. Finally, a third government policy, which is normally employed if spillover benefits are excessively large, is government financing of the good or service, and in the extreme case, government ownership and operation of the enterprise.

Present educational policies in contemporary free market economies generally combine all three government sponsored remedies for dealing with the problems associated with education. Compulsory education legislation, requiring school attendance to some prescribed minimum age, is characteristic of modern systems. Government subsidies take on a variety of forms from grants, scholarships, and tuition-waivers at universities to school lunch programs, state provided textbooks and public transportation at the elementary level. However, by far the greatest measure of government involvement in education is through the

142

direct ownership and financial maintenance of schools at all levels of educational attainment. Provision of education by the state without direct charge to the student, coupled with compulsory education laws is thought by many political economists to be the final solution to assure the consumption of education in socially desirable amounts.

AN ALTERNATE VIEW

However, there are some contemporary writers who do not agree with the mainstream view. Milton Friedman is an outspoken advocate of the removal of government from the educational realm to the extent practicable. He considers the overwhelming presence of government in education to be the chief cause of the poor quality of instruction received. Without market incentives, educational suppliers are destined to supply irrelevant and inferior educational services, Friedman holds. Furthermore, Friedman denies that "parents, especially those who are poor and have little education themselves, have little interest in their children's education and no competence to choose for them." "That, he says, is a gratuitous insult."[9] In addition, Friedman believes that research in the United States and Britain has proven that "compulsory attendance at schools is not necessary to achieve that minimum standard of literacy and knowledge." needed for societal stability in a democracy.[10] He maintains that parents are aware of the benefits of basic education and do not have to be forced to demand it. In the contemporary educational experience, the discrepancies between the quality of schooling in various areas serves to enhance income disparities, not to provide equal income distribution, he asserts. Finally, Friedman questions the idea that increasing human capital investment is a valid reason for state involvement in higher education. He writes: "If higher education improves the economic productivity of individuals, they can capture that improvement through earnings, so they have a private incentive to get the training."[11] Therefore, Friedman concludes that the purposes usually given for government interference in the educational process are neither based on sound reasoning nor on a clear examination of the facts.[12]

Other contemporary writers concur with Friedman that educational provision of today is in need of vast change. E. G. West finds especial fault with the financing of current education. He writes, "The tradition of 'free' education is a false one because it misinforms the public and it creates serious illusions." West continues, "Moreover, its strongest supporters in the past have not been the general public but special interest groups on the supply side of education, such as teachers and administrator organizations."[13] Leonard Read addresses the problem of uniformity in state education. He avers that, "Our public schooling

143

system stems from the desire and determination of some people to mold the rest of us into their image." He is opposed to this because he strongly feels that "each individual is unique, and his needs and interests are in a constant state of flux."[14] Joseph R. Peden sadly predicts the "effective" disappearance of " ... private schooling within several decades." He observes that "the social and economic dynamics of the public school system often appear to operate under a Gresham's Law - the public or free driving out the private and paid ... ."[15]

There are several changes proposed for the present system of state run education. One suggestion is a user tax scheme.[16] Since all people pay taxes, even the poorest are now paying for education for everyone. If there were a user tax, instead of property or sales taxes earmarked for education, the recipients of education would pay in relation to the amount of the service consumed. Additionally, if there were a special case where the payment were too burdensome, the state could issue long term loans or loan guarantees to the parents of public school users to help them finance their children's education over a period of years.

The most popular alternative suggestion is the voucher scheme. In this plan the government would still "pay" for education through taxes collected, but parents would control education through market power. Parents would be given vouchers redeemable for a maximum sum per child if spent on an "approved" educational service. Parents would be free to choose the educational institution which they felt was best for their children. Educational services would be supplied by profit motivated private enterprises or by nonprofit institutions of various kinds. The role of government would be limited to assuring that the schools met minimum standards of approval.[17] This plan is similar to the G I Bill instituted in the United States after World War II which allowed servicemen to continue their education at whatever institution they liked as long as the institution was approved by the government. Advocates of the voucher scheme believe that it could work at all levels of education, elementary, secondary, and at the university level.

THE INFLUENCE OF THE CLASSICALS ON TODAY'S THINKERS

The modern position on government in education was first clearly articulated by J. B. Say, reiterated by J. S. Mill, and reformulated by Henry Sidgwick. These economists were as unequivocal in their thoughts on the necessity of government in education as many of the writers of today. All three classicals identified the public goods nature of education which cast doubt on the free market production of education in quantities sufficient

144

enough to maximize social welfare. Moreover, they anticipated increases in national output from a more productive, intelligent workforce. Mill and Sidgwick both distrusted the actions of un-educated parents and were in favor of paternalistic legislation to bring about parental cooperation. All three held that marked differences in the socio-economic status of individuals could be lessened through universal basic education.

In order to internalize the externalities of education, many modern economists assume that compulsory education laws are essential. Most of the classicals at least felt uncomfortable with the idea of compulsory education although most eventually agreed to it, albeit sometimes as a temporary measure. This calm accep-tance of so strong a violation of individual liberty was made solely because the classicals believed strongly in the power of education to affect widespread social and economic change and because they accepted, even as strongly, the concept of the inability of the uneducated to value education. However, this classical view must be contrasted with Smith's ideas on compulsion which are defi-nitely more commonplace than philosophical. He maintained that if compulsion were necessary, the fault lay in the supply of edu-cation, not the demand for it. Spencer extended this thinking by pointing to the futility of forcing a child's character into developing freely through a compulsory and regulated school experience.

It is interesting that it is basically the early classicals, Smith and Malthus, who suggest alternatives to compulsory edu-cation. They both favored a test of competency in reading, writ-ing, and simple sums as a check on the child's level of educa-tional achievement. This test was not a check on the school's ability to teach, as was proposed by John Stuart Mill and is mandated today in many states of the United States. Rather, the test would determine if the individual had mastered the simple basic academic skills and was, therefore, able to take his place as an adult in society. The classicals held that the individual should be able to acquire the knowledge necessary to pass this test in whatever way he could. A modern variation of the know-ledge test is the General Equivalency Diploma (GED). The GED is a "certificate" of knowledge acquired, similar to that proposed by Mill, which an individual may obtain through testing if he does not complete the stipulated requirements for graduation at a con-ventional secondary school. The GED does not replace compul-sory attendance at school, however, and is a contemporary concession to the idea that learning can be acquired in other places than the formal education system.

Discussions about the rights of children are often heard today. Two classicals, Senior and Spencer, stood on opposite sides of the issue. Senior felt, as many current economists and other social thinkers do, that children have a right to education. Additionally, he held that to refuse a child education was to deny the mind food; as the child's body was abused from not having physical food, his mind was abused from the lack of mental nourishment. Spencer refuted this position since he held that the lack of education did not reduce the individual's liberty. He maintained that the individual was still free to pursue his way in life with or without education furnished by his elders.

The classicals, unlike many contemporary economists, offered a variety of suggestions about educational supply. Smith directed the movement toward the free market provision of education. Realizing that incentives and competition are important to direct suppliers toward consumer satisfaction in any market, Smith insisted that teachers' salaries be tied to their performance at work. The easiest way to do this, he judged, was through pupil payments for services rendered. Bentham, also, believed that quality education could be provided through profit seeking entrepreneurs. He devised two schemes, one built on philanthropy and one built on profit taking, and he anticipated successful educational supply under both methods. Humboldt, the Prussian minister of education, did not think that educational provision was exclusively in the public domain. He firmly believed in the possibility of practical private provision.

Where and how education should take place was also discussed by classical authors. Humboldt, like James Mill, was very cognizant of the role of domestic education in the formation of character. In opposition to Owenite thinking, both Humboldt and Mill stressed the importance of the early home environment in the true education of the individual. Although Marx was against any type of domestic education, he strongly favored work mixed with schooling during the student's day. Unlike Bentham's "Industry Houses," Marx's plan combined work and learning for all students, not just for the poor. Moreover, Marx was not concerned with making profit, as Bentham was, but with providing pupils with what he conceived to be the best educational methodology. Some church related schools today espouse the same belief in the efficacy of a work oriented school environment. Typically these schools entwine agricultural production with academic advance.

Most of the classical economists were concerned with two problems of educational supply which are not discussed at all today. The first issue was the cost of universal education. The early writers were adamant: what was universally provided must be cheaply provided. This is a consideration that has faded from importance in the minds of economic writers steeped in a tradition of federal subsidies to education combined with deficit spending. In the nineteenth century, the Lancasterian method of monitorial teaching was claimed to be the most cost effective way of reaching

146

many pupils without incurring large expenses. This method is still partly employed in schools today in the form of student teachers and teacher aids in elementary and secondary schools and graduate teaching assistants in colleges.

The second problem perceived by the classicals which is no longer considered relevant by today's economists is the subject matter to be covered, especially in secondary schools and universities. Marx, of all the classical writers, was most insistent upon the need for instruction in subjects that would be useful in earning a living. Many of the early economists suggested the addition of scientific and technical subjects into the nineteenth century curriculum for higher education. The effect of a steady diet of Latin and Greek on the mind was objected to most strenuously by Bastiat who felt that the study of these subjects led to anarchy. While not finding the Latin curriculum as offensive as Bastiat did, most classical writers demanded a movement toward modernization in the subjects taught in secondary schools and universities to keep abreast of (or to anticipate) changes in the industrial climate. Today curriculum change essentially has been moved to the domain of education specialists where contemporary economists are willing to let it stay. In addition, the discussion of the place of religion in education is far from complete; but, again, economists are eager to be free from intellectual involvement in this thorny social issue.

Decades after Adam Smith, the classical economists became increasingly accustomed to the inevitability of governmental educational provision. However, most would specify that government should be one of three competing systems. Those parents who preferred private or religious schools should be allowed to use them, the classicals thought. Moreover, state supply of education should not be permitted to drive private suppliers out of the market through the financial advantage received through state aid. McCulloch and Senior both proposed financial plans to help support the diversity of schools. McCulloch's plan, in some ways, was similar to Friedman's voucher scheme. The grant system of Parliament provided grants for all schools which met certain standards and would allow parents to choose the most appropriate school for their children. Students would still pay modest fees for their schooling, so reward would be tied to excellence in teaching. McCulloch's grant system would keep free market elements but would provide financial support for all schools through the public purse. Senior, perhaps the strongest advocate of the need for immediate government involvement in education, desired that those who paid tuition for private or religious schools should have a corresponding reduction in their taxes. This monetary encouragement was viewed by Senior as a way to keep the demand for nonpublic education strong enough to insure variety in educational provision.

147

Perhaps the biggest difference in the educational thought of today's traditional economists and those who wrote one hundred years ago is the lack of fear - fear of what government provided education would bring to society. Nineteenth century economists feared that universal education would fit all men into the same mold and perhaps not a desirable one, at that. John Stuart Mill forewarned of the impending propensity toward mediocrity. Those that held fast to the concepts of social Darwinism feared that the government's efforts at education would be fruitless at best, and at worse would upset the natural order. Fawcett warned, that those who accepted government educational hand-outs must be identified as paupers. The psychological stigma of pauperism was all that kept the bread lines (and the public school lines) from becoming infinitely long, he feared.

Bastiat and Spencer saw no difference between government supply of education and government supply of the other necessities of life. Food, clothing, housing, all were more essential than education. If the government felt compelled to provide education because it was so necessary to the orderly functioning of society, then surely food and clothes and housing would fit under the umbrella of government provision. Spencer feared the unleashing of government interference into all areas of life. He dreaded the effect of a monolithic governmental authority on a free market society. Bastiat envisioned a future state in which everything was free - freely provided by government with the tax revenues taken from unwitting citizens. This free provision would mean total lack of consumer choice, the complete abolition of personal liberty in consumer decision-making.

Many classicals anticipated the injustice which a system of universal education would bring. If universal education were not a necessity, then some classical writers considered taxes taken for such an expenditure to be unjust. Also, if some parents had two children in public schools and other parents had twelve, equal taxes levied for education would provide unequal returns to these different sets of parents.

Finally, many economists of the classical period were afraid of the economic consequences of reducing the costs of child rearing. Freed from the responsibility of furnishing their children with education, parents came to rely on government financial help to bring up their offspring. With the costs of raising children reduced, parents would tend to bear more children. Since the pressures of excessive population were painfully obvious in the London slums, the classical economists were apprehensive about the approval of any government policy which threatened to make them worse.

Were the fears of the classical economists unfounded? The

sameness in the curriculum of the elementary and secondary schools today has often been cited as a cause of student boredom and of early withdrawal from the educational stream. If a student does not have the same talents and interests as prescribed by the educational authorities, he is, nevertheless, condemned to be subjected to the legislated indoctrination of the classroom or be labeled a "special student." It is often the more intelligent student who finds the least satisfaction from the contemporary supply of education. This strongly suggests that John Stuart Mill's and his father's fear of universal education molding youth and promoting mediocrity was not without foundation.

The feeling that government provision of education would open the doors to government involvement throughout society has also proven to be accurate. It was not long before governments were taking liberties with their new role in society. In England, which had been the last stronghold against government involvement in education, by 1907 the government was supplying free meals for poor children, recreation centers, and medical examinations for all public school pupils.[18] In Scotland, by the Education Act of 1908 government's domain was extended through education into other aspects of life to an even further degree. Three provisions of the Scotch act were outstanding in scope: (1) children in outlying parts of the county could be conveyed to school or, if necessary, boarded nearby, (2) neglectful parents could be prosecuted where a child attended school in a dirty or verminous condition or was unable through lack of food and clothing to take advantage of the education provided, and (3) food and clothing could be provided for children in need.[19] From the provision of education to the provision of the home environment which enhances the educational experience was a very short step for many European governments. The classical economists' anticipation of these results was not in error.

Friedman has written of the injustice which accompanies the unequal educational opportunities which characterize the present system of public educational provision.[20] Although all are taxed, the quality of education to the poor is substantially lower than that which other classes receive. Additionally, those who do choose to send their children to nonpublic schools pay twice – once in school tuition and a second time in school taxes for services they do not use. Although these injustices are as obvious in today's system of education as was the fear of them in classical times, little has been done to rectify them.

The classical fear of population increase due to government provision of education and other "necessary" goods and services has also been vindicated in conditions in today's society. Few would question the assertion that government financial aid encourages welfare recipients to have more children. As the cost of

149

rearing an additional child declines because of government payments in the form of food or education or housing or medical care, the quantity demanded of children rises. The simplest economic analysis that was so apparent to the classical political economists of two centuries ago seems to have eluded contemporary policy makers in Western society.

In sum, much of what mainstream economists write about education today can be traced through the writings of the classical political economists of the late eighteenth and early nineteenth centuries. The temper of these writers' antigovernment arguments eventually softened under political pressure to ameliorate some of the social ills of a growing industrial society. However, the classical economists did not repudiate their cherished beliefs without issuing caveats and warnings; a few stood tall in their free market faith, cautioning their listeners about veering from the straight and narrow nongovernmental path. These admonitions and prognostications of disaster have all too much relevance to the state of education in contemporary society. Current conditions have summoned voices of opposition to the system of educational provision today. These voices have a familiar classical ring.

NOTES

1. Campbell R. McConnell, *Economics*, 9th ed. (New York, 1984), p. 81.

2. McConnell mentions the classic example of a lighthouse as a spillover good which would naturally be underproduced in a profit-motivated system. The problem of collecting for the light as it guides ships safely around harbors would dissuade private providers from entering this business. The lighthouse example was first examined by John Stuart Mill, expanded by Henry Sidgwick, and finally, pirated by A. C. Pigou. See: Margaret G. O'Donnell, "Pigou: An Extension of Sidgwickian Thought," *History of Political Economy*, Vol. II (4), pp. 588-605.

3. See: Martin Bronfenbrenner, Werner Sichel, and Wayland Gardner, *Economics* (Boston, 1984).

4. At the college level, the rate of return is estimated to be between 7 and 10 percent, whereas the return to the eighth year of schooling is 22 percent. See: Bronfenbrenner, Sichel, and Gardner, and Robert L. Heilbronner and Lester

C. Thurow, *The Economic Problem*, 7th ed. (Englewood Cliffs, N. J., 1984).

5. Heilbronner and Thurow, p. 481.

6. Ralph T. Byrnes and Gerald W. Stone, *Economics*, 2nd ed., (Glenview, Ill., 1984), p. 683.

7. Richard G. Lipsey, Peter O. Steiner, and Douglas D. Purvis, *Economics*, 7th ed. (New York, 1984), p. 440.

8. Ibid.

9. Milton and Rose Friedman, *Free to Choose* (New York, 1980), p. 160.

10. Ibid., p. 162.

11. Ibid., p. 179.

12. Friedman, examining the encroachment of government in education, envisioned it this way: "Though the arguments were all pitched in terms of the public interest, much of the support of teachers and administrators for the public school movement derived from narrow self-interest. They expected to enjoy greater certainty of employment, greater assurance that their salaries would be paid, and a greater degree of control if government rather than parents were the immediate paymaster;" see: *Free to Choose*, p. 153.

13. E. G. West, *Nonpublic School Aid* (Lexington, Mass., 1975), p. 35.

14. Leonard E. Read, "A Case for Educational Freedom," (Menlo Park, Cal., 1978), p. 1.

15. Joseph R. Peden, "Education and the Political Community," (Menlo Park, Cal., 1977), p. 25.

16. See: West, *Nonpublic School Aid*.

17. See: Milton Friedman, "The Role of Government in Education" in *Economics and the Public Interest*, ed. Robert A. Solo (Rutgers, N. J., 1955).

18. James Mulhern, *A History of Education* (New York, 1946), p. 453.

19. Reference Division of British Information Services, *Education in Britain* (New York, 1966), p. 60.

20.   See: Friedman, *Free to Choose*, Chapter 6.

INDEX

Abstinence theory, 56

Apprenticeship, 3, 9, 55, 71, 82–84, 97, 98, 114, 125

Attendance, 3, 9, 52, 58, 67, 68, 117

Bain, Alexander, 30

Bastiat, Claude Frederic, 6, 13, 78–79, 85–86, 98, 109–110, 121–123, 127, 132, 136, 147, 148

Dr. Bell, 17, 90, 96

Benthem, Jeremy, 8, 12, 22, 23, 37, 54–55, 56, 75–76, 80, 85, 95–98, 106, 107, 108, 120, 123, 125, 146

"Bildung," 123

"bon scolaire," 101

bourgeoisie, 13, 26, 27, 42, 57, 83–84, 91, 104, 132

Bray, Thomas, 7

British and Foreign School Society, 7, 9

Brynes and Stone, 142

Cambridge, 84

Carlyle, 23

Chrestomathia, 54–55, 75–76, 95–96, 108, 124

Compulsory education, 4, 5, 7, 10, 12, 61, 65, 70, 80, 94, 106, 117, 118, 126, 127, 128, 131, 133–134, 142, 143, 145

Cost, 7, 75, 95–97, 105–106, 118, 120, 121, 122, 134, 146–147

Crime, 28, 36, 37, 40, 43–44

Curriculum, 2, 3, 21, 23, 65, 75, 85, 86, 94, 98, 105–110, 114, 134, 147, 149

Dame schools, 2, 3, 15, 70

Democracy, 36, 38, 40–41, 143

Distributive justice, 133–134

Domestic education, 19, 20, 26, 29, 77, 78, 106, 109, 146

East India Company, 30, 97

Education Act (Scotland, 1908), 149

Elementary Education Act of 1870, 9

Elizabethan Statute of Artificers, 82

Endowed schools, 2, 62, 65, 71–73, 106, 117

Engles, Friedrich, 13, 26–27, 28, 40, 42, 45–46, 57–58, 64, 83–84, 91, 103–104, 131

English education, 7, 10, 70–71, 84

Environment, role of, 8, 21, 28, 29

Ethology, 29–30, 33

The Factory Act (1802) (The Health and Morals of Apprentices Act), 9

The Factory Act (1833), 9, 99, 103, 104

Fawcett, Henry, 10, 14, 46, 58, 104, 106, 132–133, 148

Ferry Law of 1882, 7

Foley, Thomas, 71

"Free" education, 6, 7, 101, 103, 118, 121, 125, 131, 134, 136, 138, 143

French education, 5–7, 69–70, 85–86, 87, 91, 98, 127

Norway system, 95, 124

Old Swinford Hospital School, 71

Opportunity cost, 12, 51, 58-61, 94, 117, 130

Owen, Robert, 8, 76, 146

Oxford, 73, 84

Paine, Tom, 101, 112

Panopticon, 96

Parental indifference, 61, 62, 117

Paternalism, 133-134

Peden, Joseph R., 144

Philanthropy, 8, 79, 80-81

Place, Francis, 96

Poetry, 22-23, 109

Political education, 21

Poor Law legislation, 76, 119

Population, 37, 38, 41, 56, 107, 119-120, 128, 138, 148, 149

Principles of Association, 21, 30, 125

Queen's College, 85

Raikes, Robert, 7

Read, Leonard, 143

Religious instruction, 2, 3, 4, 36, 70, 75, 88, 95, 100, 105-106, 107, 117, 124, 147

Revolution, 27, 44, 104, 110, 128

Ricardo, David, 8, 12, 13, 23, 38, 41, 54, 76-77, 96, 119-120, 128, 132

Rights of children, 12, 51, 61, 62, 142, 145-146

Rothbard, Murray, 44

Rousseau, Jean Jacques, 6, 18

Sanitary conditions, 46, 51, 108

Say, Jean Baptiste, 6, 13, 38-39, 55, 102, 107, 120-121, 144

Scotch education, 4, 69, 94, 99, 149

Senior, Nassau W., 9, 13, 39-40, 56-57, 60-61, 62-63, 64, 80, 100-101, 103, 105-106, 130, 133, 145-146, 147

Sidgwick, Henry, 10, 14, 46, 80-82, 133-135, 144-145, 150

Smith, Adam, 4, 6, 12, 15, 19, 20, 26, 28, 36-37, 38, 45, 52-54, 55, 56, 57, 59, 64-65, 69, 72, 73, 74, 76, 78, 79, 81, 82-83, 84-85, 86, 93-95, 106, 107, 118-119, 120, 125, 145, 146, 147

Social education, 20, 21

Socialist (Socialism), 8, 110, 128

"Socialist institutes," 83

Society for Promoting Christian Knowledge, 7

Society for the Support and Encouragement of Sunday Schools in the Different Counties of England, 7

Spencer, Herbert, 10, 12, 13, 27-28, 43-45, 61, 63, 64, 73, 77, 98-99, 127-129, 133, 145-146, 148

Stationery state, 38

Student fees (Tuition charge), 5, 42, 69, 71, 73, 74, 75, 86, 93-94, 102, 118, 124, 129, 146, 147

Supervisors, 74, 76

Taylor, Harriet, 42, 49

Technical training, 20, 72, 81, 82-84, 104, 132

Mrs. Trimmer, 82, 90